MY MOST MEMORABLE MATCHES

My Most Memorable Matches

FRED TRUEMAN

with Don Mosey

Cartoons by Roy Ullyet

ARROW BOOKS

Arrow Books Limited
17-21 Conway Street, London W1P 6JD

An imprint of the Hutchinson Publishing Group

London Melbourne Sydney Auckland
Johannesburg and agencies throughout
the world

First published by Stanley Paul 1982
Arrow edition 1985

Printed and bound in Great Britain by
Anchor Brendon Limited, Tiptree, Essex

ISBN 0 09 940920 8

Contents

Acknowledgements

My special thanks to Don Mosey, a personal friend, who knows me better than most people. He is a true professional and I found it particularly easy to work with him. Equally, my thanks to that great cartoonist and friend Roy Ullyett.

F.S.T.

Photographic acknowledgements

The publishers and author wish to thank the following for permission to use copyright photographs: Adrian Murrell/All-Sport; Central Press; Patrick Eagar; Press Association; Sport & General; Syndication International.

Introduction

I have always likened cricket in Yorkshire to rugby in Wales. It's as near to religion as you can get. So to *play* for Yorkshire is the highest attainment of anyone born within the broad acres. From the first dawning consciousness that I had some aptitude for the game I never wanted to play for anyone else; I have travelled to most parts of the world but I have never wanted to *live* anywhere else.

There are people in towns and villages up and down the Ridings who have never been inside one of the grounds where county cricket is played, yet who devour each detail of every match as hungrily as if they were ever-present spectators. That is why passions rise to such a fever pitch when controversy stirs in Yorkshire cricket circles.

Cricket in my county has shuffled sadly through the seventies and entered the eighties in yet another undignified exhibition of internal strife. The rest of the cricketing world looked on in wonderment as a county with the greatest traditions in the game tore itself apart. But don't be misled by it. Yorkshire cricket will rise again to be a force capable of beating touring sides and winning more championships – make no mistake about that. What has gone before means too much to too many people for it to be thrown away by the petty and self-seeking.

But this book is not about Yorkshire cricket specifically and certainly it is not about controversy. It is about the joy of playing, the fun of playing, about the memories which remain for ever to enrich the lives of those who were privileged to take part – at any level – in the greatest game of all.

I've seen him somewhere before and he certainly isn't DANNY LA RUE
CABARET * FREDDIE TRUEMAN
RAY ULLYETT.

1 The First Step

Roche Abbey v Sheffield League XI – Maltby Craggs, 1947

At birth I weighed 14 lb 1 oz. By the time I first played for Yorkshire, at Cambridge University in 1949, I had reached the age of eighteen and weighed about 10 stone so you might say my earlier physical development was in a backward direction! At the peak of my bowling career my best weight was around 13 stone 9 lb and I had a chest measurement of 46 inches so things improved a bit in my twenties.

Like everyone else born in Yorkshire in the 1930s (and before, but sadly not quite everyone afterwards) I played cricket on any spare ground I could find and always before, during and after each day at school. That was first at Stainton, then at Maltby, both in the same area of South Yorkshire, and while they might not rank high in the list of English beauty spots, at least they were well clear of a town of any size.

All my life I have disliked towns, something I probably inherited from my father and from his father. Both were stud grooms, who had dealt with horses from their earliest years, and were used to green fields and pastures. My father trained horses for Captain Adcock at Stainton Woodhouse and one of my earliest memories is of looking at a picture of him with a stallion called Baby. But the twenties and thirties brought an ever-increasing number of motorcars, the horse-*less* carriage, and the opportunities for those who wanted only to spend their lives with horses declined in natural ratio. My father was forced to take a job in the mines. He never complained, but I remember vividly the day he was able to retire. He was sixty-five on the Wednesday or Thursday and on the day shift (6 a.m. to

2 p.m.). He didn't wait until the week end – he came home just after two o'clock on his sixty-fifth birthday, took his pit clothes out to the backyard and burned them. I have often thought of the traumatic effect upon my father of having to go and work underground after a life under the skies and in the lush meadows of a training stables. But he had a wife and seven children, of whom I was the fourth, and *they* could not live simply on a love of the countryside.

My first cricket club was Roche Abbey, taking its name from one of the ruins that Cromwell knocked about a bit, and as kids we were shown Bullertree Farm where Noll sited his cannon.

It was a side of modest pretensions, run by a dear old chap called Mr Obell, but it was village cricket in every sense of the word. We played only friendly matches; during the tea interval we each had a plate containing two sandwiches and a bun, all home-made by wives and mothers (and girlfriends if they wanted to graduate to a status higher than girlfriend). The Roche Abbey wicket, at the foot of Maltby Craggs, could not be described with any degree of accuracy as perfect. My brother Arthur, a useful opening batsman, played in the side with me, and another pair of brothers, the Skeldings, included John, our wicketkeeper. It was from him I received the first piece of cricketing advice I can ever remember: 'If tha can pitch t'ball just outside t'off stump,' he said, 'it's a natural break-back.'

That was one way of putting it. In fact the hillside on which the wicket was pitched was so precipitous that any ball pitching against it could break not only 'back' but almost anywhere on the field. But in principle the advice was sound and in the first four matches of 1947 I took 25 wickets for 37 runs.

The big day came when we faced the might of a Sheffield League side on the ground under Maltby Craggs, far better opposition than any I had so far encountered. I didn't, to be perfectly honest about it, understand much at all about the game of cricket. I just wanted to bowl, and I *could* get people out, so the suggestion that our visitors might present greater problems to me made no impact at all. We batted first and were all out for 42. That in itself was no great surprise. Such things did happen and we didn't get 250 every week by any means. So tea, sandwiches and a bun were just as pleasant as usual to me. My father, however, had noticed that only two or three of the Sheffield players were still in their whites; the others had changed, clearly ready for an early return to the big city. My father, perhaps deciding on a touch of psychology or perhaps having genuine confidence in his lads (my brother Arthur had got 20 odd of our 42 runs) gently suggested to the visiting captain, 'You're not playing on a Sheffield League wicket today, you know. You might find yourself lad-licked.' It's a choice phrase, lad-licked. Well, the Sheffield skipper obviously hadn't encountered it before because he asked what Dad meant and was told, 'There's a young lad here who can make it move around a bit and you could just find yourselves in a bit o'bother.'

I imagine that the reply to this was accompanied by a faintly patronizing smile. 'I don't think so. Our openers put on over a hundred last week and there shouldn't really be any problem in knocking off the runs we need here.'

'We'll see,' said my dad.

Half an hour later the Sheffield side were all out 11, F. S. Trueman returning 6 for 1. Now that was the first step along the road to my cricketing life . . . one which at the time I hadn't even dreamt about. I had never given a thought to cricket as a career. Playing it a bit higher up the scale – yes. Making a mark in loftier cricketing realms – maybe. But getting paid for playing – never. Making a full-time career of it – impossible. Yet I had taken the first step, playing for Roche Abbey on the less-than-perfect slopes of Maltby Craggs.

The captain from Sheffield asked who the lad was and my father revealed his personal involvement. 'He should be playing in better cricket than this,' said the skipper and went back home to talk to Cyril Turner. Cyril, who had been an all-rounder in Brian Sellers' pre-war Yorkshire side, was now professional at Bramall Lane and an important link in that chain which led from the lowliest echelons of cricket in the county up to the Olympian heights. I had completely forgotten the words of the Sheffield captain if, in fact, I had ever taken any notice of them at the time. There was always another match and more bowling to be done, and I liked bowling.

The Saturday after I had, unknowingly, taken the first step, I took eight wickets against Brecks Lane and the Saturday after that Cyril Turner came to watch me bowl at Herringthorpe Valley playing fields, just outside Rotherham. That was the second step because the following Tuesday night the membership of Sheffield United, which had been closed, was reopened to admit the sixteen-year-old, less-than-10 stone F. S. Trueman. Two weeks later I played for United's Second XI and took 6 for 11 against a steel company's team, and the Tuesday evening after that I performed before a distinguished gallery of critics: Norman Yardley, the Yorkshire captain; Arthur Mitchell, the county coach; Ronnie Aspinall, one of the opening bowlers, and Cyril Turner. The third step.

From there it was a natural progression through the Federation side (in effect, Yorkshire's third team which comes together during the schools' long summer vacation) and finally into action at Fenners on 11 May 1949. F.S.T. had arrived. It wasn't all plain sailing from there, of course, because moving from League cricket to the first-class game you have to a very large extent to learn your trade all over again. I might have been gifted with a naturally sound cartwheel action but that didn't automatically make me a perfect bowler. I had to start learning to think my cricket. It took me a long time to stop expecting the stumps to go flying every ball. I had to learn how and when to bowl the bouncer (and when *not* to bowl it). I had to learn all about life itself and especially that life was different in West End hotels from life in the small communities which had always formed my environment. And I had to learn to get on with people from different backgrounds and with different outlooks.

Some lessons took longer to learn than others. There are those who will say that some were never learned at all. But one thing they can't say is that I didn't learn my trade thoroughly and ply it fairly usefully over twenty seasons. I am proud that

Bill Bowes, who took an undersized, underweight, completely raw fast-bowling prospect into the nets at Headingley, was able to say, 'He was the ideal pupil – not only desperately anxious to learn but unquestionably obedient and untiring in practice.' With that to start my career, and with one or two impressive figures at the end of it, I reckon I can say 'Cobblers' to the knockers who can only look for something to carp about from the years between.

2 The Lord's Debut

Yorkshire v Minor Counties – Lord's, 1949

To every cricketer, everywhere in the world, Lord's has a special significance. It is the headquarters of cricket. It is where the laws are made and re-made, where decisions are taken which affect every one of us, where the unique feudalism of the game rubs shoulders with the shouting and singing multitudes of Cup Final days, where the Long Room enshrines the history of the game, where formal dress is obligatory and yet where an umpire was manhandled by an MCC member during the Centenary Test of 1980. Sir Neville Cardus, with his gift for an anecdote which paints a vivid picture with a dozen words or so, recounts the arrival of two workmen during the final game of 1939, to place a green baize cloth over one of the Long Room busts – Grace, I think it was – and to carry it out. One venerable member turned to another and in hushed tones murmured, 'Did you see that, sir? That means war!' And in the years which followed, Lord's is where thousands of RAF aircrew trainees signed their first forms, took their first examinations and drew their first pay. In the stately blocks of flats which line Prince Albert Road, those wartime erks scrubbed the floors of their first billets and marched to the restaurant of the London Zoo in Regents Park for their first RAF meal.

It was not until nearly four years after the war had ended that I paid my first visit to Lord's, and I nearly missed that. In the first month of my first-class career I had played against both Cambridge and Oxford universities, against Surrey, and against Lancashire in my first Roses match. I then received notice to present myself at Lord's to play for Yorkshire – not against Middlesex, not even against MCC, but against a Minor Counties XI. I had been to London just once – the previous year (that was 1948) passing through with the Yorkshire Federation touring team. I remember seeing the Houses of Parliament and Big Ben and that was about all. Now I was to play at cricket's headquarters; it didn't matter very much who the game was against.

I cannot in all honesty claim to have been a very sophisticated young cricketer; indeed, I was raw in the extreme. Frank Stainton, one of the best of the journalists who spent their summers reporting every Yorkshire match, recorded in 1949 my first visit to a London cinema. The film was *The Snake Pit*, which won Olivia de Havilland an Oscar for her performance in that rather harrowing story of a mental institution. Apparently the subtleties of the title eluded the ingenuous Trueman of eighteen summers and I went expecting to see a more literal interpretation. Consequently, wrote Frank, I returned to the team's hotel complaining bitterly that 'I hadn't seen a single snake all the way through the damned film.' A more personal recollection would probably be the price of a cinema seat in London compared with the Grand Cinema, Maltby, or even the increasing number of picture palaces of Sheffield. Anyway, to recount that adventure in the team's hotel, first I had to *find* the hotel, which brings me back to the point when I set off for London in that June of 1949.

The message from Yorkshire's headquarters in Leeds had omitted one vital piece of information – where to join the team. So after taking a train from Doncaster – the old LNER route which used to speed down the eastern counties of England – I arrived at King's Cross without the faintest idea of where to go next. All I knew was that I had to present myself at Lords the following morning. I had five or six quid in my pocket to last me for the duration of the game – hotel, meals, travel (makes you smile a bit these days, doesn't it?) – and one piece of advice in my head, When in doubt, ask a London bobby – they are unfailingly helpful. Well, I'm sure the one I asked *would* have been helpful if it had been possible but his training course had not equipped him to tell a young hopeful from Yorkshire where to find his team-mates. Still, there was always the London cabby – he might be a bit crafty when it came to telling you the fare but he always knew his way around. So I found one who *thought* he knew where Yorkshire stayed on their visits to London, and he drove me to the Bonnington Hotel in Southampton Row, WC2. Unfortunately, his information was a bit out of date because although the county sides *used* to stay there, they had now switched to the Great Western Hotel, which in W2 was some distance away. In any case I had no means of knowing about the switch so we cruised around WC2 inquiring at one hotel after another (and there are a helluva lot of them in WC2) with the taximeter clocking up the fare at an alarming rate. Finally I decided to cut my losses and back we went to the Bonnington where I stayed the night. Next morning I made damn sure I knew which bus went past Lord's because my first London taxi ride had cost me about thirty bob.

A quarter of my resources had melted away and I hadn't even found my team yet. I found them, of course, at Lord's and Norman Yardley greeted me, 'Oh you've got here, have you?' So I had to start on a longish explanation of my adventure since receiving the message to join the side in London. 'All right,' said the skipper. 'You're here now so sit down, have a cup of tea and calm yourself.'

I walked out onto the balcony and looked around the headquarters of world cricket, the stage on which every player wants to perform. Naive and unworldly I might have been, but I can remember walking out there to bowl for the first time as clearly as if it were yesterday, and that memory will never leave me. During the three days there I explored every room and corridor and staircase. I remember the lunches at Lord's as being the best I have ever eaten anywhere in the world and I remember my instructions in the note telling me I was playing there, 'A suit, or sports jacket and flannels, must be worn and when going to lunch you will wear a blazer over your whites.' Yorkshire's secretary might not have been completely on the ball about where I was to rest my head before the game but he was taking no chances of the new recruit being turned away for being improperly dressed!

That game goes into my book of memories not because of my taxi-driven adventures or my cinema visit but for the Minor Counties' second innings. Norman Yardley bowled me right through and in my first nine overs, up to lunch, I had taken 5 for 30. After the break I got the next three and visions of an 'all-ten' performance on my first appearance at Lord's began to take shape. It was an indescribably exciting prospect. At the other end was Alan Mason, one of the slow left-arm bowlers who competed for that most essential and traditional of roles in the Yorkshire attack; a role which was wide open after the tragic loss of Hedley Verity, killed in Sicily during the war, followed by the spectacular success and quick retirement of Arthur Booth after it. Alan was a good bowler and might well have made the job his own but finally it went to Johnny Wardle who carried on the finest traditions of Yorkshire's slow left-armer.

But it was Alan Mason at the other end from me at Lord's, and between overs he joined in the general encouragement I was getting from everyone. 'Keep going, Freddie,' he said. 'I'll bowl wide of the off stump so you give it all you've got for the last two wickets.' The best-laid schemes . . . true to his word, Alan bowled wide of the off stump but we had reckoned without a tail-ender deciding to chance his arm. He played an ambitious shot at a wide ball, dragged it onto his stumps and my dream was shattered. Alan, nearly as disappointed as I was, said, 'Hard luck. I suppose I might as well bowl properly now.' And he got the last man – first ball! I was left to ponder on what might have been.

My final figures were 8 for 70 and at least I had made my mark. I was still a fairly slight figure and Bill Edrich wrote that England might now have a new fast bowling prospect if I could be built up by a few helpings of roast beef and Yorkshire pudding.

3 The Indian Summer

England v India – Old Trafford, 1952

In the last week of May 1952 the England selectors sprang two major surprises upon an unsuspecting cricket world. They appointed Len Hutton as England's first professional Test captain and they sent a message to a disbelieving aircraftman working in the sports stores at the RAF Station, Hemswell, in Lincolnshire, to report to Headingley for the first Test against India on 5 June.

Leonard might have received his news a little more calmly than I received mine. Certainly he would have reacted more phlegmatically because when the phone rang in my stores I laughed at the caller, dismissed him as a crank and hung up! Come to think of it, it was probably one of those newspapermen who never seemed to be quite on my side during my career. He must have thought, 'What an ignorant sod,' and retained the impression throughout the rest of his working life. It could have been Jim Swanton, I suppose, though he, of course, would never permit himself such a vulgar reaction, even in his thoughts! Anyway, the phone rang again a few minutes later and this time it was Bill Bowes, my old coach at Yorkshire who was now cricket correspondent of the *Yorkshire Evening News*, asking 'for a quote'.

'What about?' I asked.

'You've been chosen to play for England at Headingley next Thursday,' said Bill, and the quote he got was a whoop of delight that a war-painted Cherokee chief would have envied.

Next, the station commander, Group Captain Jim Warfield, sent for me and said Norman Yardley had been in touch with him. They knew each other from wartime service and in fact Jim was a fine cricketer himself who, I think, might have captained Leicestershire after the war if he had not stayed on to make the RAF his career. He said, 'You have been chosen to play at Headingley and I've agreed to release you on one condition.' My heart jerked a little. Suppose there was a snag about giving me leave? Was I due to be posted? Had some forgotten transgression recently come to light? I waited, thoughts flickering through my mind, dreading the thought that that 'one condition' might be one which could not be fulfilled. Was I going to be unable to play in a Test match? Jim grinned. 'The condition is this – that my wife and I get a couple of tickets so we can watch you play.' Suddenly it was a beautiful May morning again.

It was quite a cricket week for me because over the weekend before the Test – Whit weekend – I was playing for Yorkshire in the Roses match at Headingley, so on the day after that I joined an England party for the first time – in the Prince of Wales Hotel, Harrogate. My first England team dinner, the first team talk, and then, on Thursday morning, my first bowl in a Test match.

Things weren't quite right at the beginning – I bowled up the hill and Alec Bedser bowled down it from the Kirkstall Lane end. That didn't seem quite right at all! However, I duly got my first Test wicket, that of 'Polly' Umrigar who was destined to pop up in my sights once or twice in his career. On this occasion he was caught by Godfrey Evans and India were 42 for 3 but V. L. Manjrekar made a maiden first-class hundred and put on a record 222 for the fourth wicket with his skipper, V. S. Hazare, who was a fine player for India for a long time. India totalled 293 and we topped this by 41 with F.S.T., in his first Test innings, recording 0* in the undignified position of number eleven. We put things right in the second innings as far as the bowling was concerned and I got the downslope. When they went in on Saturday evening the Headingley scoreboard became the most photographed of all time: India 0 for 4 wickets. I bowled a little bit quick that evening, they tell me.

Over the years, various arguments have raged about demon bowlers of every generation. Bowlers have been electronically timed, photographed with slow-motion cameras, God knows what has been tried to sort out who is or was quicker than who. But when you come right down to it, speed bowling is all about who is on the receiving end. The batsman is the only man who can say who was quicker *to him*. It can depend upon the pace of the pitch, the age of the ball, the bounce, the light, the state of the game . . . but in the last analysis it all boils down to how that ball arrives at the batsman's end. Upon that depends whether he will tell his round-eyed grandchildren of the breath-taking pace of Lillee or Thomson or Hall or Griffith or Holding or Roberts or Lindwall or Miller or Statham or Trueman. Then someone who never faced a bowler quicker than Derek Underwood will leap in and want to know, 'But what about Spofforth or Kortright or Larwood?'

And you can turn round and reply, 'There was an underarm bowler called Smith who played for Surrey who sent one down so fast that it beat the wicketkeeper and the long stop, went through a coat thrown by a spectator and killed a dog.'

That's a recorded story and I think it goes to show that it's all relative. The Indians had not encountered anything like me and it gave me a head start against them. My first objective in life was to bowl people out and I made no major effort to disguise the fact; so when I had taken seven of their wickets in my first Test, and eight in the second, I think it's reasonable to assume they weren't too happy when I showed up at Old Trafford on 17 July. Leonard won the toss and scored 104. Trueman, number eleven, did not bat.

With interruptions for rain and bad light the England innings was declared at 347 for 9 on the Saturday morning. The pitch was wet, I'd had a couple of days' light duty and I was now rather anxious that Yorkshire should make its mark in the bowling of this Test as Leonard had started us off with his batting. Alec Bedser bowled the first over from the City end and Vinoo Mankad drove his first ball through the covers for four and leg-glanced the last ball for what he expected to be another.

But there was our debutant, Tony Lock, throwing himself forward at short leg to touch a ball for the first time in Test cricket – and to hang on to it. Right, I thought, there are still nine of 'em left, and launched into my run from the Stretford end. The captain had set me a field of three slips, three gullies, a silly point and two short legs – God, it looked good. With a shiny new ball in my hand, a totally attacking field waiting to pounce, the knowledge that the Indians must have been brooding a bit since the first and second Tests, I felt like a bomb which was ready to explode. I gave it all I'd got. In my first spell of four overs Pankaj Roy was caught at slip, Adhikari at slip and Phadkar at gulley. The catching was magnificent. Every time the ball was edged, or it lifted, it went to hand and everyone held on.

I wasn't satisfied; I wanted to see the stumps go down and Polly Umrigar seemed to provide the ideal target. He didn't like the situation one little bit and as I turned at the end of my run Tony Lock, at leg slip, called to him, 'Hey, Polly. D'you mind going back? I can't see the bowler coming in.' Polly moved – but in the other direction because as I ran in I could see Tony between the stumps and the batsman! The panic had obviously set in earlier because Dattu Phadkar actually charged towards me, swinging the bat from way outside the line, and he carved it to David Sheppard. Panic, once begun, is quick to spread and the more it spread the quicker I bowled. When I knocked over Umrigar's stumps one bail broke and pieces of it carried to just short of the boundary at the City end.

When the broken piece had been retrieved and a new bail substituted, the umpire, Dai Davies, handed it to me and as we went in to lunch I handed it to my brother, Arthur, who was sitting with my father in front of the pavilion. He had it mounted in a little showcase and to this day nothing would induce him to part with it.

I didn't worry too much at the time about why the Indians were bowled out for 58; I was too delighted with 8 for 31 for that. But they simply didn't get in line. Not everyone does today and that is something the coaches have to sort out.

Duggie Padgett, who is in charge of Headingley, said to me not long ago, 'I used to go in to bat *prepared* to be hit in the ribs. It didn't matter who was bowling. If he got one through it was going to hit you – *if you were in line*.'

Perhaps that morning at Old Trafford, and a lot of other occasions when a fast bowler has run through a side, is best summed up by Herbert Sutcliffe, to me the Master, and one of the best players of fast bowling of all time. He once sat talking to me in my garden and said, 'Some batsmen can play fast bowling, Freddie, and some can't. But if they all told the truth, no one *likes* to play fast bowling.'

I think perhaps that sums it up rather well.

4 The Mutinous Erk

Combined Services v The Australians – Kingston, 1953

It will probably come as a surprise to one or two people to learn that I loved nearly every minute of my two years' national service in the RAF. I was proud to be a part of a great service in the first place. I made a lot of good friends, real friends, and I enjoyed a lot of good sport as well – and not simply cricket.

While association football is not my favourite game and I don't think I would walk across the street to watch a present-day professional match because of the crowd behaviour, I always enjoyed playing it as a youngster just I have always enjoyed most games. It was while I was playing for the RAF at Hemswell, in Lincolnshire, that dear old Bill Anderson, then manager of Lincoln City, came up to have a look at me and invited me to play at Sincil Bank as a result. Perhaps I might best be described in modern parlance as 'a bustling type of forward'. Anyway, either at centre forward or out on the right wing I could usually manage to get in the thick of things and that was fine by me. At the time I was an up-and-coming fast bowler with England so I suppose there was a certain amount of interest for people in seeing how I performed on the football field; it was said at the time that Lincoln City's second team 'gates' with Aircraftman Trueman in action were twice those the first team enjoyed at their Third Division matches.

It all got a certain amount of publicity, which I don't suppose did Lincoln City any harm and I was glad for Bill Anderson, who went right through into the sixties when he was the longest-serving manager (at one club) in the Football League – longer even than Matt Busby – which was all right in my book because he was a great fellow. But the publicity went to all quarters, of course, and one or two people began to point out to me the risks to my cricket career if I was injured. So I packed up soccer. I was sorry to have to do it, but at the same time I am not exactly sorry I decided to concentrate on cricket.

If it comes as a surprise to learn that I enjoyed national service, let me go a bit further and say I wish it were still with us today because I am a firm believer in discipline. Those who were shaken by my first statement might now be falling about at the second but it's perfectly true none the less.

A lot of people *think* they know me and, over the years, a hell of a lot have *claimed* to know me. Hence a whole string of stories about what I am supposed to have done on this tour and that and what I am alleged to have said to this person and that. My friends, people who really do know me, have to spend half their lives challenging the most outrageous tales trotted out by blokes I have never met but who go on at dinners and cricket society meetings as if it were all gospel truth.

So I am branded the eternal rebel, the man who delights in bucking authority. It's absolute bull and it makes me more angry than anything else. So, I repeat: I believe in discipline. And I am in no way hedging my bets if I qualify that by saying I believe there is a right way and a wrong way of *administering* discipline. Authority should not be lightly bestowed and so it should not be wielded irresponsibly. Respect is something which has to be earned rather than automatically accorded to someone in authority, whether it is in the services or civilian life. Of course, by the very nature of service life one comes up against authority rather more frequently and so one encounters the two extremes with some regularity – those who are natural commanders and those who are not.

National service in the early fifties brought together a lot of good sportsmen, professional sportsmen, and inevitably a lot of them took the field under the captaincy of *amateurs*. Well, most of us were used to that in professional cricket and amateur captains gained respect (or failed to do so) as much by their character and personality as by their playing ability. Service cricket carried this just a little further because there were always going to be one or two senior officers around who not only fancied themselves as players but who fancied even more cracking the whip over the backs of pros. By and large, though, the dressing room was a pretty democratic place. We didn't spring to attention every time we were addressed by the skipper, for instance, but the very fact that most of us were professionals provided a built-in sense of order and organization.

I have often wondered what happens in the *extremely* democratic regions of a rugby front row when A/C Plonk, the hooker, has sweated blood to win a strike against the head only to find Pilot Officer Prune, his tight-head, kicking it back to the opposition!

Well, it takes all sorts, and in service cricket of the early fifties we had all sorts and conditions of men – Ray Illingworth, Terry Spencer, Jim Parks, Peter Sainsbury, Freddie Titmus, Brian Close. And we had all sorts of conditions of officers, too.

My own skipper in the RAF was Alan Shirreff, a great bloke and a very useful all-round cricketer who played at one time or another for Cambridge University, Kent, Hampshire and Somerset, depending (I expect) on where he was stationed as a regular officer. Under his captaincy we had a good side and a good time. Not all service captains were like Alan Shirreff. Some were like Lieutenant Commander M. L. Y. Ainsworth, of the Royal Navy and Worcestershire.

I had played against him once and he contrived 40 odd runs through and over the slips after which he rather frequently expressed the view in the wardroom that F. S. Trueman wasn't very much of a bowler. Lieutenant Commander Ainsworth was in charge of the Combined Services XI to play the 1953 Australians at Kingston in a match for service charities. Amongst his flock was A/C Trueman.

We had won the Ashes at the Oval and in my second season of Test cricket I was becoming established as a specialist short fine-leg fieldsman. When I had bowled the opening over I walked to leg slip for Terry Spencer only to be imperiously dismissed to deep fine leg by Commander Ainsworth. As diffidently as I could, I pointed out that if England regarded me as a specialist in my position it was not unreasonable to expect I could do the Combined Services a bit of good there as well.

'Not at all,' replied our gallant commander. 'Major Parnaby always fields at short fine leg.' So Aircraftman Trueman trudged morosely to the boundary edge. It is stretching it a bit to say that he did so in a disgruntled manner but it is certainly true that he was far from gruntled.

A certain morbid satisfaction was possible when one K. R. Miller edged a catch to the major off Terry Spencer which was not taken. But that vicarious pleasure evaporated as Miller went on to score a big double hundred – a career best of 262. The major did not excel in his specialist position and another 202 followed from Jim De Courcy, the New South Walian with the patrician name and the plebeian calling of boiler-maker. By now it would be fair to say I *was* disgruntled and between the periods when I was called upon to ply my trade I found a seat on the base of the sightscreen.

The commander was not pleased and it showed. I was not pleased and that was reasonably apparent, too. I don't think Major Parnaby was entirely ecstatic with the way the day had gone but at least he had been vouchsafed his favourite spot in the field!

At the end of the game the skipper of the Combined Services addressed himself to the mutinous erk. 'Trueman,' he barked in tones which no doubt caused strong men to blanch on the quarter-deck, 'you will never play again for Combined Services.'

'Correct, sir,' I replied briskly. 'Quite correct.'

'I beg your pardon?' queried the commander, no doubt taken at least slightly aback by this ready compliance.

'You are absolutely right, sir. I was demobilized two days ago but I stayed on to play in this game because it was for service charities.'

I would have rather liked to encounter Lieutenant Commander M. L. Y. Ainsworth in a Yorkshire v Worcestershire match but, sadly, I never did.

5 The Ashes Return

England v Australia – The Oval, 1953

Coronation Year, 1953, was quite notable in many ways. First of all there was the coronation itself and as an ardent royalist I have no difficulty in remembering that summer. And although the first four Tests all ended in draws there was something noteworthy about all of them. The first, at Trent Bridge, saw Australia reach 244 for 3 and then collapse on a rain-affected wicket to 249 all out with Alec Bedser taking 7 for 55. And as Big Al followed up with 7 for 44 in the second innings I've no doubt that one or two of the Australians will remember it as well, especially young Richie Benaud, on his first tour. In the second innings he was bowled round the back of his legs by Bedser's leg cutter and I think he could be forgiven for shaking his head in disbelief.

The second Test, at Lord's, gave Trevor Bailey a place in the record books and one high on the Aussies' hate list as he stayed for four and a quarter hours with Willie Watson to save a game which seemed completely lost when the first three England wickets went down in the second innings for 12 runs. At Old Trafford, less than half the scheduled time was available because of rain and who knows how that might have turned out had not Australia, after gaining a first-innings lead of 42, crashed to 31 for 8 in their second (Wardle 4 for 7). Then it was Bailey again at Headingley, helping materially to save the game by bowling wide down the leg side to a defensive on-side field. This time he went one better than the record book – he went into the statute book because the restriction of on-side field-placing stemmed directly from this game.

And so to the Oval. Australia had held the Ashes for 18 years and 362 days when they finally changed hands on 19 August 1953, and it was one of the great moments of my life to be in the side when it happened. I had not had a good season, partly because I had developed ankle trouble through pounding down on some of the matting-covered concrete wickets we used in service cricket (I was doing national service in the RAF at the time), and partly because I was unable to play regular first-class cricket during that service.

It was my first Test of the season so I was naturally all keyed up and someone somewhere was fancying me too, because a story came back to our hotel that a bookmaker had offered odds of a hundred to one against my getting a wicket in my first two overs. A Trueman fan had had a quid's worth on this so he stood to win £100 (a heck of a lot of money in 1953; if I could do my stuff. Do you know, Denis Compton dropped Arthur Morris in my *first* over and Denis was normally a very safe catcher. Somewhere there's a bloke who's been cursing him for twenty-eight years and wondering what he might have done with £100.

After that miss I didn't really get into the game until Lindsay Hassett and Neil Harvey had put on 66 for the third wicket. I had been watching Harvey closely, especially after being warned by Len Hutton (who created some sort of record himself in that series – losing the toss five times but winning the series) that Neil was a good hooker and not to give him a chance to play the stroke. I decided that if I could bowl it short enough to tempt the hook, but far enough outside the off stump to make it a bit chancey, I might be able to find that extra yard of pace to induce a mishook. Well, it worked. Neil didn't hit it plumb and the ball soared higher and higher, drifting towards mid-wicket. The skipper himself had to run round to make the catch and it was a good one but I'm pretty sure he was more than a little happy to feel it in his hands. I felt a bit better myself, remembering what he had said about feeding the hook shot. Len's delight was so apparent as he clutched the ball that Peter May said to him, 'You look as though you've just had a week at Blackpool.'

Another remark in that game sticks in my mind and it had a great significance for me. I had bowled a slower ball to Arthur Morris earlier in the innings and Ray Lindwall said to me later, 'You are going to be a *thinking* bowler. I can see that . . . the changes of pace, trying something new.' Now that meant a tremendous amount to me. Lindwall was my hero. He had rampaged through England in 1948; he was one of the great bowlers of his age and with Ray in partnership with Keith Miller, Bill Johnston or Alan Davidson (and sometimes both) to follow up no wonder we had struggled. So I spent a lot of time talking bowling to R. R. Lindwall. I also talked to any fast bowler who would talk to me. I pursued them into corners – Miller, Bowes, Perks, Butler, Lambert, Gover, Jackson. If they had just one grain of knowledge or experience that I could use, I wanted it. I thirsted for information; I pursued tired bowlers at the end of the day in search of it. I haunted them. Since I retired, in 1968, only a couple of fast bowlers have ever come to ask me for advice, Dennis Lillee being one of them.

But back at the Oval. Lindwall got 62 in that Australian first innings and but for that we might have got home earlier. Eventually I had him caught by Godfrey Evans to give me four wickets in the innings and when we managed to lead Australia by 31 we were working into a position to win because the wicket was going to turn in the second innings. Why so sure? Well, have a look at the results at the Oval in the fifties and then remember that Laker and Lock were in our side!

Now in those days the England team stayed at the Great Western Hotel in Paddington and on what proved to be the final day of that final Test of 1953 I came out of the hotel with Hutton and saw the newsvendor who had a stand near the hotel. On one of his boards he had drawn a fair approximation of the Ashes urn and underneath was printed, 'They're Ours!'

As we passed he looked up, waved and shouted, 'Good luck.' He might have been a little bit premature but in the event he was justified because Laker and Lock bowled Australia out for 162 and we won by eight wickets. The Ashes *were* ours after just three days short of nineteen years. I wish I could have gone back to see our newsvendor supporter's little tribute officially on display but a certain amount of celebration was called for.

Nevertheless that is one of the little touches that I have never forgotten. It is the sort of thing which is the very essence of cricket . . . the sort of thing which enables one to look back across the years and smile a smile of sheer pleasure.

That's cricket. Life itself can be less kind. My maternal grandmother, to whom I was deeply attached and from whom I took my middle name, Sewards, was two hundred miles away in Yorkshire. She told my dad and my mother, 'I'm going to bed. I'm a little bit tired, but at least I've seen us win back the Ashes.' And with that she died.

6 The Matting Wicket

West Indies v England – Trinidad, 1954

Apart from Jamaica, at the opposite end of the Caribbean, Trinidad is the largest of the West Indian islands and probably the most cosmopolitan with Dutch, French, Portuguese, German, Indian and Chinese amongst its ethnic influences in addition to British and African.

This produces some startlingly attractive girls, a rather easy-going approach to life and at least one major contribution to cricket's terminology. Ellis Achong, the Test spinner of the thirties, made his debut at Queen's Park Oval, Port of Spain, on 1 February 1930, and as his first Test wicket claimed the genial Patsy Hendren, bowled for 77. Patsy had gone in with England at 3 for 2 wickets which very quickly became 12 for 3 and his innings saved a rather tricky situation, but this did not lessen his self-reproach at being clean bowled by a somewhat unorthodox and certainly unexpected delivery from a Test debutant. He returned to the dressing room muttering disgustedly, 'Bowled by a bloody Chinaman,' and cricket acquired a new technical term. More than twenty years later, Ellis Achong was to leave an equally deep impression upon the members of an England touring side, not least of all upon me.

Let's look at the ground first of all. Queen's Park Oval is perhaps the best-equipped of the West Indian grounds with double-deck stands surrounding most of the playing area. Players, press and the spectators in adjoining stands on the south side of the ground look over the field to a dramatic back-drop of the spectacularly shaped Northern Hills which

THE TEST SO FAR
RAMADHIN! ENGLAND OUT!
Roy Ullyett.

provide, really, the only outstanding topographical feature of the whole island.

Trinidadians are volatile, artistic, fun-loving and – strangely, perhaps, in such a mixed society – intensely patriotic, especially when it comes to their cricket teams. England's 1981 tourists found this to a remarkable degree when the West Indian selectors left out Deryck Murray from the Test side resulting in a) a major boycott of the first Test and b) a minor riot amongst those who attended the game. Clive Lloyd, the captain, was barracked all the way to the middle for the toss and again when he went out to bat as Trinidad wrote a sad chapter in the history of West Indian cricket.

The island gave us the calypso which was already an age-old musical art form when it was dramatically introduced to England in 1950 by the legendary Lord Kitchener (a calypsonian, not a warlord) through those 'two little pals of mine, Ramadhin and Valentine'. And Trinidad gave us the steel band – providing anything from frenzied Afro-Caribbean rhythms to stately classics beaten out on hollowed-out oil drums. Just as the March Festival, Trinidad's major tourist attraction, brings joyous processions, marathon 'pan' sessions and original compositions by the score, so a concert at the Port of Spain Queen's Hall by the Catelli All Stars Steel Band can provide a unique musical experience with the works of Mendelssohn, Schubert and Mozart.

In the cricketing sense Trinidad has its own pronounced characteristics, too. It rarely, if ever, produces swashbuckling batsmen of the Barbadian/Antiguan type and its bowlers do not follow the jet-propelled flight of the Jamaicans or smaller islanders. Just as a European influence is present in Trinidadian batting – Stollmeyer, Gomes – so we find Oriental wiles more often present in the island's bowling.

The mysteries of Sonny Ramadhin were recreated thirty years later by Harold Joseph who went on the 1981–2 winter tour to Australia with his marvellous variety of right-hand finger spin – no fewer than six variations, as reported by England's batsmen the previous winter, all delivered out of the *front* of the hand. And it is to Trinidad that the West Indies selectors have turned so often when spin, orthodox or eccentric, was deemed necessary for the international attack.

While this is no doubt due, in part, to national characteristics, the heart-breakingly slow wickets must have had a part to play, too. And touring bowlers, watching the shin-high bounce of the sixties, seventies and eighties, perhaps inspecting sore spinning fingers, too, might well reflect that it was even worse in earlier decades – on those deadliest of bowling killers, jute matting pitches. I had my first (and, thank God, my last) experience of these in March 1954.

The West Indies had gone two up in the series by winning the first Test at Sabina Park, Kingston, by 140 runs and the second at Kensington Oval, Barbados, by 181 runs.

At Bourda, the Test ground of Guyana (which was then British Guiana, incidentally), Len Hutton, skippering England, had scored 169 and Alf Valentine had taken his hundredth Test wicket, at the age of twenty-three, but we won by nine wickets. Riots at games in the West Indies are fairly commonplace and this was no exception because when a eighth-wicket stand in the Windies' first innings ended in the run-out a shower of bottles and other objects were hurled onto the ground. Anyway, we went to Trinidad now only 2–1 down and I had my first taste of bowling on jute matting: 33 for 3, 131 for 1.

Jeff Stollmeyer, whose family have been prominent businessmen in Trinidad for generations, was captain of the West Indies. He won the toss and decided to bat. 'Bat' may not be precisely the right word because when they declared we needed 532 to save the follow-on! We made it with five runs to spare which may explain why the West Indian bowlers were not noticeably keener on the matting wicket then we were. Stollmeyer opened with J. K. Holt and their scores of 41 and 40 respectively represented failure in relation to what was to come because their departure landed us with the three Ws – Everton Weekes, Frank Worrell and Clyde Walcott.

First came Weekes at number three: a great guy, Everton de Courcy Weekes, a nice man, a great pal of mine and a magnificent batsman. But on this occasion, just a trifle fortunate, I think. When he was 10 or 11 I got one to find the edge and it went through to Dick Spooner, the Warwickshire wicketkeeper/batsman, who was in because Godfrey Evans was troubled by a boil on his neck. We all went up with the appeal but 'not out' said the umpire. Ten runs or so later, Everton got another touch to the wicketkeeper and again we all went up. Not out. Trevor Bailey got him to touch one and again the verdict was 'not out'. It was unbelievable. Eventually, Everton reached 206 when he was c Bailey b Lock and as he walked past me on his way to the pavilion, at last, I grinned at him, 'Well played, Everton. Not bad, two hundred and six for four innings.' He grinned back.

'Five,' he said. 'I got a nick when I was in the sixties but nobody bothered to appeal.' I suppose by that time we all had a sense of futility about appealing.

Frankie Worrell represented no cause for concern. The senior players had said to me (just a little disenchanted with bowling conditions – after all, I had taken the first wicket, Holt's, rather a long time ago and it was now 430 for 3): 'Don't worry about Worrell, Freddie. He's right out of form.' It was probably as well for us that he was because he got only 167 and put on 338 with Weekes! And there was still Clyde Walcott to come. He managed a mere 124 so the three Ws between them had scored 497 and even though they were all three Barbadians, and despite the intense rivalry which exists between the various sides *within* the West Indies, a collection was organized in the crowd for the benefit of the three of them – not a 'Benefit' as we get in this country, but simply a spontaneous gesture of appreciation to three great batsmen. Nevertheless, I felt that the man who ought to have had the collection was the number six batsman, Bruce Pairaudeau.

Another nice man, Bruce (who afterwards made his home in New Zealand) was not a bad player, but on this occasion was run out for 0 in a scorecard which read Holt 40, Stollmeyer 41, Weekes 206, Worrell 167, Walcott 124 – and a number seven, Denis Atkinson 74. Run out 0 is bad enough at the best of times. Run out 0 in the middle of that little lot was not too good. But worst of all, Bruce was run out going for a third run by one of my flat throws, 70 yards from the boundary and right over the top of the stumps, I'm glad to say. Somehow it helped to make up for that 1 for 131.

The sequence of incidents in that first innings was not yet finished. Towards the end of the innings Denis Compton was bowling, got a 'Chinaman' to turn and it was nicked to Tom Graveney at slip. Even after some of the decisions we had experienced we were absolutely staggered to find the batsman given 'not out'. The umpire was none other than Ellis Achong, Patsy Hendren's Chinaman of twenty-four years before. Maybe he regarded that particular delivery as his copyright but it was 'not out'. Graveney hurled the ball down in disgust and here we come to one of those instances of 'giving a dog a bad name' which have not exactly helped my career in various aspects of the game over so many years. That evening, at a cocktail party someone remarked 'how disgusting it was for Trueman to have thrown down the ball in a rage'.

Tom Graveney heard this, stepped in and said, 'Hold on a minute. That was me, not Freddie.' But the mud has stuck. History marks me as the offender.

Yes, I remember the fourth Test at Port of Spain, Trinidad, all right. I think most of us will remember it in one way or another because just about all the members of the party took some part in it except Godfrey Evans. Two of our substitute fieldsmen at one time or another (Kenny Suttle and Alan Moss) took catches. Denis Compton had the best bowling figures with 2 for 40; Jim Laker split his face wide open, above and below one eye, trying to hook a fast bowler called King (who, after four days of toil on the matting, was the only one interested in trying to bowl flat out). The man with most sense was Brian Statham who retired with a strained side after nine overs of the West Indies first innings and didn't bowl again, lucky chap. In their second innings, they reversed the roles of McWatt, who hadn't taken a wicketkeeping catch in our first innings, and Ferguson who had bowled 47 overs, taking 1 for

155. Both must have reflected that the switch might profitably have been made one innings earlier because McWatt-the-bowler took 1 for 16 and Ferguson-the-wicketkeeper held two catches!

The game lasted six days. No Test had ever been finished on Queen's Park's jute since it was laid more than twenty years earlier and we didn't spoil that record. The match produced 1528 runs and just 25 wickets fell.

7 The County Championship

Yorkshire v Sussex – Hove, 1959

The story of Yorkshire's return to County Championship success in 1959 is very much tied up with the story of Ronnie Burnet's captaincy for two years; in some ways a controversial and strife-torn two years but in others a time of unexpected honour and glory. Brian Close, in his autobiography, has been violently critical of Ronnie; Ray Illingworth, on the other hand, paid the highest of tributes to the last of the amateur captains in *his* life story. So, as I start to look at the events leading up to Yorkshire v Sussex at Hove on 1 September 1959, perhaps this is the time for the third member of the triumvirate to chuck in his twopenn'orth. The Trueman vote comes down very firmly indeed *for* J. R. Burnet.

Ronnie was born a few months before the end of the First World War so he was getting on for forty when he was called up to skipper Yorkshire after ten seasons in the wilderness. Ten years without an honour was unheard of in the broad acres up to that point in the club's history. Things have taken a very sorry turn for the worse since then, but that is altogether another story.

In 1958 desperation at our continued lack of success walked hand in hand with incredulity because, man for man, that Yorkshire side of the 1950s must have represented the greatest assembly of pure talent ever to play under the White Rose banner. And it never won a single thing. Just consider the players: Hutton, Lowson, Wilson, Lester, Halliday, Watson, Yardley, Close, Appleyard, Coxon, Brennan, Wardle, Trueman. Then start to think of some of the blokes who couldn't get into the side, men who would *walk* into it today but who in the fifties had to emigrate to other counties: Johnny Whitehead, who was as quick as most people who have ever played the game and who left for Worcestershire; Jackie Firth, a great wicketkeeper as well as a great character, who went to Leicestershire; Ken Smales, a good off spinner who went to Nottinghamshire; Freddie Jakeman, a lovely batsman who played for Northamptonshire; Norman Horner (Warwickshire); Arnold Hamer – he regularly got 2000 runs a season for Derbyshire; Geoffrey Keighley, who skippered Yorkshire once or twice but languished for most of his career in the second team. It was absolutely incredible that from this immense wealth of talent we couldn't win a thing.

Recently I played a round of golf with Johnny Wardle and Bob Appleyard and suddenly, apropos of nothing at all, Wardle stopped in the middle of a fairway and said, 'What would the three of us be worth to a county today?' I hope nobody will misunderstand the nature of his remark. It was not made in any boastful sense at all. But with sixteen counties fighting to keep their overseas players and even some people in Yorkshire wondering if it is not time for *us* to import stars, I think it is a pretty reasonable question to put to the cricketing world.

In particular I believe it was an extremely pertinent point to put to some of today's practitioners who live in a dream world as far as their own ability is concerned. If you try to tell them anything they are very likely to turn round and say, 'Oh, it's a different game today. *You* would be out of your depth in present-day cricket.' I nearly throw a fit when I hear that sort of drivel. In the 1981 season a young Yorkshire bowler said something of that nature to Tony Nicholson – Nick, who was ten times the bowler the cheeky kid addressing him will ever be! I can't think of more than a handful of players in the 1980s who would have been able to cope with Lindwall and Miller, Heine and Adcock, or Trueman and Statham any better than they coped with Holding and Roberts. Nor can I think, without a great deal of difficulty, of more than two or three 1980s bowlers who would have had a price in bowling at Simpson and Harvey and Hassett and O'Neill, at Sobers, Worrell, Weekes, Walcott, Butcher and Solomon.

So Wardle's comment was a perfectly logical one as far as I was concerned. He was a great bowler even in the dynasty of Yorkshire's slow left-armers, which is a sort of cricketing *Debrett*; Appleyard, even in a career which started late and was interrupted and foreshortened by ill-health, must have been one of the great bowlers of all time. And I managed over 2300 first-class wickets. So it is not unreasonable, I think, to feel that a trio of bowlers of that calibre would, today, be able to name their own figure when signing contracts.

Norman Yardley gave up the Yorkshire captaincy after 1955 and Billy Sutcliffe took over for the next two seasons. And still we won nothing – with four or five international batsmen and four or five Test bowlers. The answer, of course, was quite simple. We had no team spirit and we didn't pull together. What to DO about it was not quite so simple.

The Yorkshire committee's choice was Ronnie Burnet, the second team captain whose main experience had been gained in the Bradford League. Now that League is and always has been a great production line for county cricket. You could probably get together a couple of good Test sides composed of men who have learned their trade within a radius of ten miles from Bradford Town Hall; but skippering a League side on a Saturday afternoon is a far cry from leading a team over three days of first-class cricket.

Long-term strategy is a complex thing and something which takes years to assimilate; it was an incredibly difficult thing the committee were asking of a thirty-nine-year-old man with no experience at all of playing in a three-day game. And all that was before one started to consider the immense problems of handling players so far ahead of him in playing ability that they were out of sight, players of vast *Test* experience, let alone county cricket, players who felt very strongly that they had forgotten more about the game than the captain would *ever* know, players of tremendously strong character and personality, players who were *convinced* they knew best, players who had defeated the attempts to pull them together as a playing unit by an experienced Test captain like Yardley and the hail-fellow-well-met, gregarious character who was Billy Sutcliffe (who was a better player than many gave him credit for). It was an Everest of a task which confronted J. R. Burnet. I had my doubts about his tactical direction but on his ability to handle the tough characters, I had none – with good reason.

During the previous season I had had a spell out of the first team and I needed some practice. I telephoned the Yorkshire secretary and asked, 'There's a Second Eleven match at Middlesbrough tomorrow. Can I play in it?'

'I'll speak to the chairman, Freddie,' said Jack Nash. 'Why do you want to play?'

'Because I want some practice,' I replied. 'I haven't been bowling for a couple of weeks.'

The reply came back from the chairman in typical terms, 'Yes, he can play. And while he's at it, tell him to take Appleyard – he needs some bowling. And Closey, as well. He needs some batting practice.'

So three Test cricketers presented themselves at Acklam Park, Middlesbrough, for duty with Yorkshire's Second XI captained by J. R. Burnet. Now I scarcely knew Ronnie, certainly not in terms of playing with him out in the middle. But I did know something else . . . that before the Second World War, when he was nineteen or twenty, Ronnie had been regarded as one of the most promising young spin bowlers in the Bradford League and, as a batsman, he had been singled out by the great George Hirst as someone with a big future. So obviously he had been able to play a bit – but that was twenty years ago.

After the war, business preoccupations resulted in his life taking a different course and he must have decided that a cricket career was not for him. But at least I knew his pedigree was good. Beyond that, I knew little or nothing about him as a man. It was not long before that gap in my education was plugged. He gave the three of us a welcome to the camp, won the toss, decided to bat and said to Closey, 'Right, Brian, you go in first.' Closey looked at him.

'I'm not going in first,' he replied.

'Oh yes you are,' said Ronnie. 'Listen to me, I'm the captain of this side and if I say you go in first, that's where you go in.' Closey still didn't like it, demurred a little, you might say, and Ronnie delivered his ultimatum: 'Either you go in first or you can go home. I don't mind which, but make up your mind . . . *now*.' Closey went in first.

He later turned his attention to me. 'I've had instructions from the committee,' he told me, 'and I don't want you to do a lot of bowling.' It was my turn to be surprised because I had asked to play so that I could get some bowling practice. I pointed this out. 'Never mind,' said J. R. Burnet. 'I want you to try five or six overs to begin with, then have a rest. After that, we'll see. . . .' I was, as I say, surprised. I didn't like it. But this chap had already shown that he was the captain and we were going to do what he wanted, whether we liked it or not. So there seemed to be no point in arguing.

'Fair enough, skipper,' I said. 'If that's what you want.' So he asked me which end I wanted, what field I wanted, set it, and I bowled six overs with the wind behind me.

Then Ronnie walked over and asked, 'How d'you feel?'

'Fine,' I replied.

'Okay, take a rest.'

'But I'm fine,' I protested. 'I feel okay to go on.'

'Take a rest,' repeated the captain. And I took a rest. But then came the moment when he had to say the same thing to Bob Appleyard. And Appleyard didn't like to take a rest. He liked to bowl all day – if that was necessary – and I'm damn sure he would have bowled all night as well if there had been anyone to bowl to.

He and Johnny Wardle had always been able to say to first-team captains 'I'm going to carry on bowling' and, believe me, they did. So the dialogue now went something like this:

'Right, put your sweater on, Bob.'

'No, I'm all right.'

'Put your sweater on just the same.'

'No, I've told you, I'm all right.'

'*Take your sweater.*'

'No, I won't.'

'Hey, you're playing with the second team now. I don't care what you do in the first team but here you do as you're told. Now *put your sweater on.*'

Now Bob and Johnny, great bowlers as they were, often carried on bowling in the county side when everyone else thought they shouldn't have been and it may, on occasions, have been a factor in our losing games. And listening to all this how's-your-father going on I thought to myself, 'Hello, if ever this feller becomes captain of Yorkshire [and there *was* some talk of Billy Sutcliffe giving up the job at the end of that season] I think one or two people are in for a rude awakening.' A disciplinarian was something new to those of us who had been playing first-team cricket through the fifties. Not everyone was going to like it if he took over the senior side. And in 1958, he did.

During the winter, when I was living in York, he knocked on my door one day and said, 'Hello, Fred. Shall we have a bottle of champagne? I've got one in the car.' I said 'yes,' first and 'why?' second. 'I've been made captain,' he said. I was delighted to join him in that bottle of bubbly.

Now they say that Ronnie was responsible for Johnny Wardle leaving Yorkshire under a cloud and I don't know how much was the captain's personal responsibility or how much sprang from committee instructions. That it was a great blow to Yorkshire, there's no doubt. Wardle was a great bowler, a fine cricketer and a fine cricket brain. He probably resented having a thirty-nine-year-old amateur, who had never played first-class cricket, placed over him. I can understand that. But Ronnie made no secret of his years, his lack of first-class experience. Neither did he try to cover up the fact that the committee had given him a specific job to do: to lick into shape a team which for ten seasons had rarely if ever performed like a team. Bob Appleyard retired in 1958 and Johnny Wardle left in that sad way in mid-season. Willie Watson had gone to Leicester, Len Hutton and Harry Halliday, together with Ted Lester, had

Wardle is fired

retired earlier in the decade. What Ronnie Burnet set out to do in his second season was to mould a side round four established players: Jimmy Binks, who was the best wicketkeeper of his day by a mile – why he did not play for England more times than he did is something I shall never understand; Brian Close, who has driven us all daft in his time but who had so much ability that if he had played regularly on good wickets he could just about have scored a century every time he batted; Raymond Illingworth, a great all-rounder; and myself, enjoying a fair degree of success at that stage of my career.

What Ronnie did for the young players in the side – Ken Taylor and Bryan Stott, who had been capped the previous year, Duggie Padgett, Brian Bolus, Philip Sharpe, Don Wilson, Jackie Birkenshaw, Bob Platt, who were all uncapped at the beginning of 1958 – was to instil into them a sense of what the game was all about and how much it meant to play for Yorkshire. He made them believe in themselves and their destiny. Above all he made sure that no one regarded himself as greater than the team; everyone played for everyone else. There was no room in Ronnie Burnet's side for prima donnas.

In 1958, the rebuilding process under way, Yorkshire finished eleventh in the championship table. By the end of June 1959, we had beaten Nottinghamshire, Glamorgan, Sussex, Warwickshire and Essex. Padgett had scored two centuries, Ken Taylor, Brian Close, Ray Illingworth, Bryan Stott and a young colt from South Yorkshire called Harold ('Dickie') Bird one each. In July we beat Derbyshire, Essex and Leicestershire despite a bad patch in which we lost to Northamptonshire and Surrey who were once again challenging for the title after seven on the trot. In August we beat Middlesex, Kent and then came to a grinding halt with defeats at Bath and Bristol. But the month ended with our beating Worcestershire before going on to Hove for the final game of the season. We had just an outside chance of the title if we could beat Sussex. They were going to give us nothing at all. In fairness to Surrey, they could not indulge in any quixotic declarations even if Robin Marlar had felt inclined to do so. I doubt if he would ever have contemplated that sort of thing against Yorkshire in any case.

The Sussex second innings dragged through the latter part of the second day, into the third morning, to lunch, and beyond that. When the last wicket fell – and 'Snarler' Marlar, like all his side, had made us work every inch of the way – we had to make 215 to win in just 103 minutes.

It was then, I'm absolutely sure, that the moment came when Ronnie Burnet felt it had all been worthwhile – all the criticism from press and public about his appointment, the dreadful trauma of the Wardle episode, the battles with the senior players and the worry about the junior ones. I wonder how he felt, sometimes, when he went to bed at night after a day that had gone wrong. Did he ever feel he should not have taken on the job of captain of Yorkshire? Did he wonder what the experienced men in the side were thinking? Did he think (and no one could have blamed him for thinking it): What the hell am I doing here, nearly forty-one, leading a crowd of lads, some of them half my age, in a game where you have to work hard physically and concentrate 100 per cent mentally, all day long?

Whatever his thoughts in the two slogging years of his captaincy, it all came right for him at about half past two on the afternoon of 1 September 1959. Just a little bit crestfallen at the time it had taken to bowl out Sussex, Ronnie came in from the field, sat down and said, 'Well, lads. I thought we had a chance of the championship if we could win this one but it's a pretty tall order.' And as one man we all voiced the same thoughts. The words might have been different but the sentiment was just the same all round the room.

'Don't worry about it, skipper. We're going to win. There's nothing for us if we *don't* win so let's set about hitting 215.'

Bryan Stott hit the first ball straight back over Ian Thomson's head for 6 and we reached 50 in 20 minutes, 100 in 43 minutes, 150 in 63 and in 95 minutes we had won by five wickets. The runs mostly came from Bryan Stott (96) and Duggie Padgett (79) but afterwards no one thought of it that way. Everyone who went in contributed something and those who didn't have a chance to go in suffered most! At one stage we thought Closey had lost us the game by hitting a ball right out of the ground and we forfeited two or three precious minutes whilst it was retrieved! I made a brief excursion to the middle . . . six, four, two, one, stumped . . . but looking back on the day, I remember Padgett's innings most of all. He scored off every ball he received and that isn't done every day, even in the John Player League. In an innings of 79 it was fantastic. In a foretaste of the John Player League, Marlar had his field right back so that there was one, sometimes two runs everywhere – and we took them. At the end Bryan Stott was absolutely knackered.

With its gift for restraint, the county's annual report that year said: 'Your Committee heartily congratulates the team upon winning the Championship and upon the entertaining cricket played throughout the season, and feels that Mr Burnet's leadership played a great part in the Team's success.' They can say that again. And again and again. It is no problem at all to recall the scene in the Hove dressing room that afternoon. It will remain in the minds of every man and boy who shared that greatest of days.

We had to travel to Scarborough that night which was one hell of a drive without motorways, but no one gave it a thought because we were taking the championship home after ten long years. And yet it wasn't just that – it was the way it had been achieved. I am absolutely convinced that at no time during that afternoon's play did any one man in the party give a single thought to himself. It was the team. It was a pleasure shared, a triumph jointly achieved, and the sheer joy of that corporate effort was felt by every member of the party. That is my abiding memory of Hove, 1959 – coupled with the name of Ronnie Burnet.

Our own opportunity to pay tribute to him came on the very day after our win at Hove. We had all slogged back through the night in our various ways to Scarborough for the first game of the Festival – Yorkshire v MCC – and Ronnie was due to play for MCC. 'Oh no you don't,' we told him. 'You have led

Wife struck in eye with breakfast kipper having just told him not to be late home for dinner as she's making a Yorkshire Pudding
Bless this house and Kennington Gas Holders in particular.
COUNTY CHAMPIONSHIP
YORKSHIRE GO TO TOP
Yorkshire
Warwick
Glamorgan
Derbyshire
Middlesex
Northants
Surrey
Essex
Pet dog. NOT a Yorkshire Terrier
PICTURE OF A RABID SURREY SUPPORTER LOOKING AT THE CRICKET CHAMPIONSHIP TABLE THROUGH DARK GLASSES AND THE WRONG END OF A TELESCOPE AS HE CAN'T BEAR TO SEE YORKSHIRE BACK ON TOP.
Roy ULLYETT

Yorkshire to the championship; now you lead the champions out to play their next game.' And Vic Wilson, destined to be Yorkshire's first professional captain although no one even dreamed it at the time, was hurriedly substituted for Ronnie in the MCC ranks and J. R. Burnet skippered Yorkshire. And quite rightly so.

8 The Roses Match

Yorkshire v Lancashire – Old Trafford, 1960

The Roses match is a unique cricketing fixture. It would be untrue to say that events at Headingley and Old Trafford during the spring and summer bank holidays have any *direct* link with the troubles of fifteenth century England and yet the indirect ties are there. The county flags, and our blazer badges, are derived from the heraldry which identified the Houses of York and Lancaster, and on the first morning of a modern Roses match it's good to see the actual flowers being worn in the lapels of rival supporters. (While it's easy enough to get the roses in August, I've often wondered about their ready availability during the May game – it must cost a bob or two to go on parade properly dressed at that time of the year.)

Perhaps the oldest story in cricket is about the southerner who ventured into a Roses encounter and his indiscriminating applause finally brought instructions from both his neighbours to 'keep out of this. It's nowt to do with thee.' And that's really the way it is. It is the one fixture a year which means more than any other to the county members and consequently it is not surprising that the legends have grown about it.

Now legends (or at least good legends) have their bases in fact and there is no shortage of fact in the stories which have been handed down. Those who saw the grim, tight-lipped battles of pre-war years will need no convincing about the truth of Emmott Robinson's terse summary of conversation on those occasions, 'We say "How do" in't morning and "Good neet" at t'close and in between we just say, "How's that?"' Emmott was the archetypal Yorkshire professional of the pre-war years and no one who met and talked cricket to him for even thirty seconds would doubt the sheer passion of his involvement in all county matches but the Roses game in particular.

It is said that he made a point of getting to one match earlier than anyone else and, having checked that no one had yet arrived in either dressing room, Emmott took a cushion, went into the showers, removed his trilby hat and knelt to pray: 'Oh Lord, I know that Thou art the great Judge of any cricket match between county or nation. Today Yorkshire and Lancashire meet in the Roses match. If Yorkshire are the better side, they'll win; if Lancashire are the better side, *they* will win [he must have said that with an utter lack of conviction]. And if there's rain it will probably be a draw. But, Oh Lord, if You will just keep out of it for three days we'll knock Holy Hell out of 'em.'

That sums up as accurately as anything can the feeling of the men who took part in Roses matches of the twenties and thirties. The war changed men and it changed their attitudes. The games of the mid- and late-forties brought together men who had spent long years serving alongside each other and it was difficult to retain the atmosphere of passionate rivalry bordering upon naked hostility.

Nevertheless, the unique atmosphere of the game itself remained. Huge crowds, starved of top-level competitive sport, still crowded into the grounds for the biannual fixtures; gates were closed before eleven o'clock on the Saturday and Monday; and the players, while exchanging a few more elaborate greetings than 'How do' and 'Good neet' were nevertheless locked in mortal combat from the moment the first ball was delivered. Personal rivalries were born and some of them stretched over the years and, in some cases, into different counties.

In the mid-seventies, Leicestershire were playing Yorkshire at Park Avenue, Bradford, and Don Oslear (later to become a Test match umpire) was having his first season of county championship cricket. Roses match blood-letting was something Don had merely read about and certainly he had no reason to expect to encounter it in a game involving Leicestershire. But Leicestershire included in their ranks Ken Higgs – not a native Lancastrian by any stretch of imagination but one who had known the heat and toil of the day in many a Yorkist-Lancastrian skirmish. And he was bowling now to a cordially hated foe, Geoffrey Boycott.

Higgs caused a few playings and missings and suddenly he was transported, no longer was he wearing the leaping fox of the hunting shires but the Red Rose which had seen the slaughter of Towton and Tewkesbury. He denounced Boycott, in the time-honoured prose of fast bowlers, as a 'spawny bastard'. Boycott's reply was not essentially conciliatory. The battle of words grew in intensity to the horrified astonishment of Umpire Oslear. He spoke to the bowler; he spoke to the batsman. Neither took the slightest notice. Finally, he spoke to the Leicestershire captain who happened to be Ray Illingworth, a man not unaccustomed to such exchanges. Illingworth nodded and walked away.

At the end of the over Illingworth strolled over to the other umpire, Cec. Pepper, and laconically suggested, 'Ask your mate not to interfere in private Roses battles, Pep.'

My earliest memory of a Roses match is one of wonderment. First of all it was only my third first-class game and the other two had been against universities. To be transported into the atmosphere of Old Trafford, 1949, from the tranquil hush of the Parks and Fenners was like flying to the moon. Sixteen or seventeen international players thronged the dressing rooms, the atmosphere in the ground was tense and highly charged, and the cricket was played with an intensity I was never to find surpassed in any Test. But for the moment it was enough to be there – playing alongside the legendary Len Hutton, every Yorkshire schoolboy's hero.

Rain delayed the start and we batted in the afternoon. At close of play, Leonard was 60 not out and next day he was given some stick in the Sunday papers. (His scoring rate might have seemed like indecent haste in a pre-war game but we now had a new generation of cricket writers who did not appreciate such matters. A not-out 60 on a rain-affected wicket was apparently something to be dismissed with contempt.)

On the Monday morning Len asked me to go out and bowl a few to him in the nets. He returned to the dressing room, changed his shirt, had a cup of tea and then went out and hit the first ball of the day straight back over Bill Roberts' head for six. He went on to make 201 of the most fantastic runs I have ever seen. In the second innings, feeling unwell, he batted lower down the order and was 96 not out when Norman Yardley declared. The man I had revered as I grew up had done his stuff for me, and in the Roses match too. Three years later, when I was called up to play in my first Test I was to breathe my silent gratitude to the Roses match because I had been a bit worried about how I would feel in the atmosphere of international cricket. I need not have worried. The pressures of Test cricket proved to be nothing like those of the game against Lancashire I had played in the previous weekend!

But of all the forty or so of those matches I experienced, the one which always springs immediately to mind is the game at Old Trafford on 30 July, 1 and 2 August 1960. Although we won the championship that year we lost twice to Lancashire, our nearest rivals in the championship, and that caused more despondency than the title brought delight.

'Noddy' Pullar, who often formed a threesome with 'George' Statham, my bowler partner and myself when we were on tour, was no mate in the Roses series. At the time he was in a very good trot which brought him a Roses average of around 70 over four seasons, and in the Whitsuntide game he had hit 121 at Headingley where we were beaten by ten wickets on a spinner's pitch.

In a summer of wretched weather we drew seven matches, won five and lost two before we went to Old Trafford itching to wipe out the memory of that defeat at Headingley. Lancashire were chasing us for the title as well, so the August bank holiday game had even more than the usual Roses significance. Again it was a rain-affected three days and Statham and Higgs bowled us out for 154 in the first innings, getting a lead of 72 largely

Well played Lancashire! Let me shake you by the NECK
YORKSHIREMAN CONGRATULATING LANCASTRIAN ON FAMOUS ROSES VICTORY OFF LAST BALL OF FINAL OVER!
ROY ULLYETT.

through the batting of Bob Barber and Alan Wharton. In our second innings we were rolled over for 149, giving Brian Statham 9 for 66 in the match. Lancashire needed only 78 to win and they had all afternoon to get them. It was the sort of situation which would prompt many counties to make a token attempt to get amongst the wickets with their front-line attack and then, as the situation became more hopeless, to introduce the more occasional bowlers to get the job over and out of the way. Not in this case. This was the Roses match.

The Lancashire spinners, Dyson, Higgs and Barber, had all taken wickets in our second innings as well as Statham and it would be alien to all Yorkshire tradition to neglect an opportunity to bowl their spinners. Indeed, I think it was Cardus who recalled meeting George Hirst and Wilfred Rhodes gloomily trudging through Regent's Park one gloriously sunny Sunday morning after a wet Saturday at Lords. 'Why so solemn,' he asked, 'on such a beautiful morning?'

'It's a grand morning all right,' muttered Rhodes sombrely. 'We were just talking about that "sticky" that's going to waste up t'road.'

So starting with spin was certainly one of the ploys discussed as we planned our campaign in the dressing room. Finally it was discarded as carrying too many risks and we decided on a pace attack, making every possible use of the lift that was in the pitch to give the batsmen as much trouble as possible, with a defensive field setting. We would try to force Lancashire into mistakes while cutting off as many scoring opportunities as possible.

We could not reasonably expect to bowl them out but we could hope to put them under pressure when they got behind the clock. Above all, we wanted to prevent a Lancashire win. Well, don't tell anybody who saw that Tuesday afternoon's play that defensive cricket can never be exciting because I'm pretty sure no one who saw it will ever forget the next two hours.

My partner was Mel Ryan, who had never had a settled place in the side and in fact played only a handful of matches each season. His experience of bowling 'tight', therefore, was limited but he bowled magnificently and although his fifteen overs cost 50 runs that wouldn't be considered particularly expensive in any other context – and he kept chipping in with a wicket as well. At the other end I think I am entitled to count that unchanged spell of sixteen overs as one of the best pieces of bowling in my career.

We set out to put Lancashire under pressure and we didn't half succeed. As wickets went down, with the target of 78 to win getting closer only by painful degrees, hopes began to rise on our side and something close to panic set in on the other. No one left the ground. On the contrary, as the news filtered back to the city centre the offices and shops of Manchester began to empty and the ground to fill. It took a man with no nerves at all, whatever the situation, to swing the pendulum slightly against us – 'Chimp' Clayton, the Lancashire wicketkeeper. He had contrived 15 runs which were worth their weight in gold but he was the non-striker when the last ball of the match came to be bowled at a quarter past five. Lancashire were 77 for 8 – the scores were level. A wicket would give us a draw; a ball that merely did not yield a run would give us a draw too.

The field was distributed with painstaking care. Everyone chipped in with advice but it was FST who had to bowl that last delivery. The batsman was Jack Dyson, an off-spinning all-rounder who also played football for Manchester City. With all due respect we knew he wasn't especially partial to quick bowling and it was all too clear that he was acutely conscious of the situation. Clayton was pacing about at the other end, wishing like mad he had the strike and giving Dyson all kinds of instructions which I'm sure Jack didn't even hear. I gave him a last lingering look before starting to walk back and I think he expected a bouncer.

That walk back took rather a long time because I was turning over in my mind the problem of what ball to bowl. Finally, I decided on that old standby, usually regarded as the classic delivery for such a situation, the yorker. I concentrated hard, started to run in, my mind filled with a picture of the bottom of the leg-and-middle stump. It was as good a yorker as I have ever bowled but Dyson countered with the only possible effective answer. He shuffled forward, bat and pad close together, and somehow he got an edge. It was an edge just thick enough to deflect the ball wide of Jimmy Binks' outstretched glove and away the ball went to the fine-leg boundary. Coldly the Yorkshire handbook records, 'Yorkshire lost by two wickets at 5.15 p.m. on the third day.' It says nothing of the drama, and the heartbreak, of one single delivery. My figures at the end of a marathon stint read: 16 overs, 4 maidens, 28 runs, 2 wickets. It was as good a spell of bowling as I ever produced in my career but I would have traded one or two more spectacular-looking Test analyses for a runs column which simply read '24' instead of '28'. That was the importance of the Roses match.

Afterwards, as I smoked a reflective pipe in a hushed and disappointed dressing room, my old mate Brian Statham came in and said, 'F.S., one of the best matches I have ever seen; certainly the best Roses match I have ever played in. And after that bowling performance by you and Mel Ryan this afternoon all I can say is, "You were bloody unlucky." '

Unlucky we might have been; gracious, certainly, was that tribute from George. And we still won the championship by 32 points – from Lancashire. But they would count their disappointment in that direction as nothing beside the delight of recording a double over the ancient enemy – as we would have done. Twenty years later I think of the 1960 season not as one when we won the championship but as the time we were beaten twice by Lancashire – and a thick edge off my last ball brought the winning runs. Such wounds are slow to heal . . .

9 The Jet Age

South Africa, 1960

On 13 September 1960, Yorkshire, as champion county, beat the Rest of England at the Oval by 137 runs. Less than twenty-four hours later I was practising in the southern part of Africa. Now in the 1970s and 1980s this had become commonplace, but to me, accustomed to *sailing* to the West Indies and South Africa for my tours, it seemed nothing less than miraculous. At the time, the world's airlines were switching from piston-engined aircraft to jetliners and I was whisked from Heathrow to what was then Rhodesia by BOAC's new marvel of modern transport, the Comet. It was a tremendous experience for me, just as it was to be en route to South Africa, a country I had never seen but about which I had heard so much – not least from that summer's tourists who had just been involved in a controversial series centring on the action of their fast bowler, Geoff Griffin.

The chance to visit South Africa came from Ron Roberts, who was by profession, I suppose, a freelance journalist but as far as cricket was concerned he was one of the finest international ambassadors the game has ever had. Ron died prematurely and that was a very sad blow indeed for the game. I sometimes wonder if much of the racial controversy which bedevilled the game in later years might have been averted if Ron had lived to carry on his tours with multi-racial sides to wherever those sides were welcome. In the 1960s they were welcome everywhere. Ron used to say that one of his hobbies was grappling with the airline timetables of the world, trying to get players from two, three and four countries together in the same place and at the same time. No one ever knew him to fail but he had a whole fund of hair-raising stories to tell about near misses!

The Cavaliers XI was to play in Rhodesia, Transvaal and Natal, and that was the second tour on a major scale organized by Ron; he had not yet got round to fully multi-racial sides, as he did later. Our party consisted of eight English and four Australian Test players and was a pretty useful combination by any standards: Tom Graveney (captain), Brian Statham, myself, Alan Moss, Kenny Barrington, Ray Illingworth, Geoff Pullar, M. J. K. Smith, Richie Benaud, Norm O'Neill, Bobby Simpson and Len Maddocks.

The match at the Oval finished at 4.20 p.m. Five members of the tour party were involved in it – Ken Barrington, Mike Smith, Alan Moss, Ray Illingworth and myself – and we had a mad dash by car to London airport to join up with the other lads, and by two o'clock in the morning we were in Khartoum. As I stepped out of the aircraft to stretch my legs during the refuelling stop, I thought someone had opened the door of a blast furnace. Although it was the middle of the night the temperature was over 100 degrees and, after leaving a crisp evening in London only a few hours before, I had never in my life experienced such a sudden change. By breakfast time we were in Salisbury and – used as I was to the leisurely rate of ocean travel – I was left to marvel that the previous afternoon I had been playing cricket 5000 miles away. Less than six months later, the speed of modern travel was to enable the Scottish RFU to blaze the trail of short tours by flying out for just three games.

We won the first game, against Rhodesia, by six wickets but my chief memory of that visit is meeting a policeman, sitting in uniform on the steps of the pavilion in Salisbury, who was destined to become one of the best uncapped bowlers of all time and my regular opening partner with Yorkshire. It was Tony Nicholson, then a trooper in the police force of Rhodesia whence his parents had emigrated following his birth in Dewsbury. 'Nick', as he became universally known in the game, had (and still has) the ripest Heavy Woollen District accent you are ever likely to hear but my first meeting with him was when he was on duty in Salisbury as guardian of the players' property in the dressing rooms! (Later, the family returned to England; Tony applied for, and was given, a trial with Yorkshire; a great lad and a fine bowler.)

We played a second game in Rhodesia, which was drawn, but Richie Benaud broke a thumb in trying to hold a hot return catch and all hell broke loose from the press of Australia because he was due to lead Australia in the series against the West Indies starting two months later. (The fact that he recovered in time to do so is a matter of history – and rather colourful history too: the first Test, in Brisbane, is the one which ended with the scores tied as Australia's last wicket fell to a run-out off the penultimate ball of the game.)

We moved on to Johannesburg for the first of two games against the Transvaal and dealt quite comfortably with the State side, winning by ten wickets. Bobby Simpson hit a superb 178 and Trueman the all-rounder came into his own with 5 for 59 and 59 runs. And then it was across to the lovely city of Durban to play Natal.

I learned that the legendary Wally Hammond lived here but was rarely seen in cricketing circles and, in fact, never went to watch the games played by Natal – which was a source of disappointment to many people. Never being shy about such things, I decided to go and visit the great man of whom I had heard and read so much. I told my room-mate ('George', of course) that I was going to see Wally Hammond and he asked, 'How?'

'Well,' I said, 'I'm going to get a taxi and ask the driver to take me to the Hammond house and I'm just going to knock and ask if I can see him.' It all seemed as straightforward as that to me.

'Okay,' said Brian, 'I'm coming with you.' And we were joined by Geoff Pullar and Ron Roberts.

The taxi duly deposited us at the Hammond home; I boldly knocked on the door and performed a mass introduction to Mrs

Hammond. I don't know whether she was surprised, shattered, or what, but she ushered us in to see the Great Man, who immediately and hospitably opened the bar in the lounge of a lovely house and the five of us sat talking cricket until the small hours.

We learned that he had one major regret about his playing days – he had no records or photographs of his friends, the men he had played with, no mementoes to remind him of the days when he was creating the legend that lives on today. So Ron Roberts undertook to get together a collection of souvenirs for him when he got back to England.

I then said, 'There's something we'd like you to do for us, and that is to come to the ground and watch some cricket.' That took a lot of persuasion because for reasons no one could ever quite discover, Hammond had become something of a recluse. But he came.

Our hosts were enraptured. Hospitality flowed. The South Africans practically swept up the dust from the ground before him as he walked in. He had lunch with us, stayed to watch the game and after that was, from time to time, a spectator at Natal games. I like to think I played a little part in coaxing back a great cricketer to a game he had never ceased to love.

At one stage it seemed that the Cavaliers might let Hammond down on his return to the cricketing fold. Natal had its share of fine players at that time: Trevor Goddard, Roy McLean and others who were more than useful cricketers. We had a lead of 45 in the first innings but collapsed in terrible style in the second and we were heading for a hefty defeat when I went out to join Mike Smith. He said, 'Get your head down, F.S., and we'll see what we can do.'

It wasn't an official first-class match so the records can't tell me exactly what my contribution was but I think it was about 60 or 70. What I do remember was that M.J.K. hit 204 out of our second-innings of 357 and by bowling out Natal for 316 we won by 86 runs. But it wasn't as easy as that. Our most successful bowler was Bobby Simpson (4 for 110 with his leg spinners) so it was obviously a pretty good wicket. It was so good that when I attempted a bouncer at Trevor Goddard he, picking up the length, ducked a long, long way. He could, I suppose, have made a career as a limbo dancer because he got down so low that the ball passed over his back and just, only just, cleared the bails. That was a bouncer on a Durban wicket.

However, for some reason or other, the wicket was entirely different in the first innings when we were out for 180 and Natal for 135. Brian Statham took five of those wickets and in Durban, in those days, they had a delightful little tradition: anyone taking five wickets in an innings was asked to plant a tree and, once planted, there it remained to grow for as long as it lived. So as far as I know there is a Brian Statham tree growing in Durban at this moment. I hope it doesn't get him banned from something or other.

We had a whale of a time in South Africa. I am not going to get involved in the politics of this or any other situation. I am, always have been, a professional sportsman and I have visited countries on that basis. To me, the South Africans were marvellous people who treated me magnificently and I judge countries on the way people behave to me. I have been back a number of times and I have never had anything but red carpet treatment. To me, it's a wonderful country.

For our last match of the tour we returned to Johannesburg where we were to play a South African Select XI. Before the game, Jackie McGlew said to me, 'You won't move it around here, F.S., as you do at home. We're six thousand feet above sea level; it's a clear atmosphere and *nobody* swings the ball here.' I don't know how he felt when they went in a second time, 96 behind, and they were 12 for 5.

The ball was swinging around all over the place! Statham and I were scything through them like mad and when number seven arrived at the wicket he brought with him a note for the captain: could the two of us be taken off because the authorities had taken a lot of money in advance bookings and they badly needed the game to go through to the next day.

Skipper Graveney obliged. The quick bowlers were removed, the slow men came on, and two men later to become well-known in England got a pile of runs – Syd O'Linn, who played for Kent, and Eddie Barlow, who went to Derbyshire towards the tail end of a great international cricket career. So the match was 'doctored' but we still managed a win by five wickets – though you wouldn't think so by looking at *Wisden*, 1961. There it is recorded that the Combined South African XI made 249 and 218 (making a total of 467 in my book), Cavaliers 345 for 8 declared and 124 for 5 (469 runs in all with five second-innings wickets left). *Wisden* says, 'Drawn.' I wonder how that happened.

And so to the last match of the tour, not a first-class match, not really an official one, but a game which Ron Roberts had been asked to squeeze in during our journey home, a one-day fixture in Kenya. Once again – it was my first visit to East Africa – I was struck by the friendliness and hospitality of everyone I met. Nairobi seemed a marvellous place to me and, after our experience in Johannesburg, I didn't worry too much about the fact that here, too, we were five or six thousand feet above sea level. In neither of those two places are you conscious of being at an altitude as you look around you. In the Alps, or the foothills of the Himalayas, it's rather different because you are surrounded by snow-capped peaks and there is no escaping the fact that you are rather closely involved with mountains. In Johannesburg and Nairobi there is no real consciousness of being at an altitude . . . until, of course, you start to get involved in any strenuous activity. Then you learn to do it in short sharp bursts.

However that wasn't the real problem as we faced a team of players mostly of Asiatic descent and we all know how wily they can be. But even allowing for that knowledge, no one was prepared for this team of international stars – Graveney, Simpson, Pullar, Smith, O'Neill, Barrington – being rolled over for 150 or so. But it happened. It was a matting wicket and no one could cope with, let alone explain, the way the ball was cut this way and that, all over the place.

However, we thought that if a team of international batsmen could be whipped out for 150 by a team of shopkeepers, at least our international bowlers could return the compliment with interest. But it didn't happen like that. When we bowled, the ball went straight on. It bounced at a uniform height. All in all, no matter who was bowling in our side, every delivery seemed to carry with it a cordial invitation to smash it to the boundary. Disaster loomed before us. An unbeaten record against the first-class cricketers of Rhodesia, Transvaal and Natal seemed certain to go by the board against a crowd of enthusiastic but totally inexperienced Kenyans of Indian and Pakistani descent.

They were more than halfway to a win with only one wicket down when I caused a bit of bother by bowling a bouncer which, to the astonishment of everyone concerned – including the batsman – *bounced*. And it hit the bloke in the mouth so he had to be rushed off to hospital. We then discovered that he was the son of one of the businessmen who had sponsored the game and he wasn't very pleased at all. I apologized to him and the casualty, as he was carted off for treatment, so we put that bit right.

It was then that it began to dawn on us that a matting wicket behaves according to the way it is pegged down. If it is drawn tight it will provide the best batting pitch you have ever seen. If, however, it is left a bit loose it will allow the ball – no, *encourage* it – to jump about and turn like mad. Still, it was a *friendly* match; it was the last game of the tour; it was one we had agreed to play as a little gesture to the cricketing public of Kenya; and our visit *was* being sponsored. So we didn't ask for the matting to be loosened. I had a little go with the cutters which I was beginning to develop at that time, got seven wickets and we won with less than a dozen runs to spare. It was a desperately near thing, but at least we'd saved face. What with that, and Trinidad six years earlier, I was quite happy never to see another matting wicket as long as I lived.

That tour left me with a whole bagful of memories. I liked bowling to South African batsmen who seemed to me to have a very positive approach to the game. They liked playing shots, which suited me because that gave me a better chance of taking wickets. It is a matter of the utmost regret to me that I never made an official MCC tour of South Africa. I would have loved to play in the glorious setting of the Newlands ground, in Cape Town, with that exquisite backdrop of Devil's Peak and Table Mountain. I would have loved to play official Test matches at the Wanderers, in Johannesburg, as well as in Durban and Port Elizabeth. But at least I can say I have played cricket in South Africa and enjoyed every minute of it.

10 The Off Cutter

England v Australia – Headingley, 1961

The summer of 1961 brought Richie Benaud's Australians to England. It brought 3019 runs from the bat of an Australian destined never to play Test cricket – Bill Alley, another of my old friends, who celebrated a testimonial year by breaking records all over the place for Somerset as he had done in Northern League cricket. It brought a first ever county championship to Hampshire under Colin Ingleby-Mackenzie; and at Repton School in Derbyshire, the captain of cricket, a young man called Richard Hutton, chose as his prize a copy of *Wisden*.

Benaud was an extremely popular captain of the tourists who promised to play attacking attractive cricket, and kept his promise. There were exciting finishes up and down the country against county sides and the first Test at Edgbaston was drawn only because England, as they had done four years earlier on the same ground, fought a tremendous rear-guard action in their second innings. In the second Test, at Lord's, we got a bit of a hiding by five wickets (even though Brian Statham and I gave them quite a shock when they wanted only 69 to win) so there were changes in the management and amongst the workers.

Peter May took over the captaincy of England from Colin Cowdrey, David Allen replaced Ray Illingworth in the off spinning department and with my front office colleague J. B. Statham suffering from a strain, that fine old trouper of the county scene, Les Jackson, came in at the age of forty.

The Australians won the toss, batted, made a solid start and reached 192 with only three wickets down. Then Jacko and I took the second new ball and seven wickets fell for the addition of the next 45 runs. Les had the first bite at the cherry from the pavilion end (that is, the *old* pavilion at Headingley – we tend now to call it the football-stand end) and I came down the hill from my favourite Kirkstall Lane end to finish with 5 for 58.

The second day was spent in consolidation by the England batsmen with Cowdrey and Geoff Pullar batting really well until Graeme McKenzie and Alan Davidson (bowling medium-paced leg cutters) polished off the innings. Still, we had a useful lead of 62. With his fifth ball of the Aussie second innings Les Jackson knocked out Colin McDonald's leg stump and then, on a wicket which was taking spin, Neil Harvey batted superbly, first with Lawry, then O'Neill.

Now, I had watched with interest Alan Davidson's use of the cutter in the early part of the day. As a left-arm fast-medium bowler (and a superb one, too) his 'cut' moved the ball from leg to off producing a fiendishly difficult delivery. I heard the batsmen talking about it and it had a special significance for me. I was in my thirteenth season, a pretty good term of office for a fast bowler, and I had always tried to think about my bowling and to try out new ideas.

Recently I had been thinking that I couldn't go on for ever bowling quick, and I had been experimenting with off cutters. In one particular game – against Glamorgan at Swansea where the wicket was nearly always a slow turner – I had had success with them, to the extent of six wickets fairly cheaply, and I thought that the Headingley pitch might be responsive to off cutters.

Our two spinners were on, Allen and Lock, and the captain decided to change them round so he asked me to bowl one over while they switched ends. I used the long run but as I came in for the third ball I decided to try a cutter. It bit and it lifted. Harvey, going for the drive because to him it looked like a normal delivery and it was well up to him, hit it straight up in the air and Ted Dexter had a long time to wait for it to come down at cover. Peter May asked me what I had done – Harvey had looked well set – and rather excitedly I told him I had tried a cutter and it had worked. Peter went over to J. T. Murray, the wicketkeeper, and checked, 'What happened?'

J.T. said, 'He bowled the cutter, it gripped and it bounced a bit as well.'

So Peter said, 'Okay, carry on.'

'I'd like to bowl them off my short run,' I told him. 'I think I can do it more accurately like that.'

'All right. If that's what you want,' the skipper said. In the space of twenty-four deliveries the cutters claimed five wickets for no runs. With just under a quarter of an hour of the third day remaining we beat Australia by eight wickets and my match analysis of 11 wickets for 88 was, and remained, my best in Test cricket. I still have the ball, nicely mounted, which produced that second-innings collapse and I remember with great pleasure that my five-for-none came as a result of *thinking* my way through a game.

It was in the nets at Headingley that I first tried a few experiments with my grip, amongst other things. The cutter was produced by placing my index finger just behind the seam (which was upright) on its left-hand side. My second finger then went round the middle of the ball – the equator if you take the seam as being a line through the poles. At the moment of release these two fingers came away quickly in a chopping or cutting action. The effect was that of a fast off break being delivered but with the additional advantage that the extra pace could induce greater bounce.

Arthur Mitchell, the chief coach, watched me experimenting in this fashion for a while and then told me, 'You know, Freddie, if you can bowl spells of that stuff there will be times when we can leave out a bowler, use you as a two-in-one, and play an extra batsman.' That was useful to the side and it was useful to me, too, because I had begun to think about the days when I could no longer rely on extreme pace as an ally to my outswingers. I was looking for a new method of attack and on Saturday, 8 July 1961, it looked as though I had found it.

YORKSHIRE, Black Thursday.
I've never known feeling run so high. At 11.30 when Test begins, 'e plans to stop suppin' ale for ½ minute as protest at selectors dropping Trueman
Roy ULLYETT

Certainly the memory lingers pleasantly with me after twenty years. With the selectors it melted away just a little earlier. For the final Test at the Oval, just forty days after taking 11 for 88, I was dropped:

11 The 200th Wicket

England v Pakistan – Lord's, 1962

The fact that in the course of sixty-seven Tests I only made tours to Australia, New Zealand and the West Indies is one of the great disappointments of my career. I would have loved to visit more cricket-playing countries because travel is and always has been one of the great pleasures of my life. I am indeed grateful that cricket has given me the opportunity to do so much of it – more, in fact, since my playing days ended than during them but still in the cause of cricket in one form or another. I was desperately disappointed to miss tours to South Africa but I have been able to make up for that even though there is no substitute for the thrill of playing Test cricket abroad. Nevertheless, I did manage to play Tests against all the cricket-playing nations, even if many of the series were at home, and it's quite remarkable how the milestones of a fairly chequered career were distributed: best analysis against India, 300th Test wicket was an Australian, 250th a New Zealander, and the 200th was a Pakistani (the Pakistan captain of 1962, in fact, Javed Burki). The 150th was a South African, Jackie McGlew.

I had started that 1962 series with a nice long rest as England won the toss in the first Test at Edgbaston and scored 544 for 5 declared. Cowdrey, who opened with Noddy Pullar, made 159 and the declaration was delayed until Peter Parfitt completed *his* century in an unfinished, record sixth-wicket partnership with David Allen of 153. Edgbaston has never been exactly a bowler's paradise and even after two days with our feet up, Brian Statham and I had to leave it largely to the spinners, Allen and Lock.

Lord's, however, where the second Test was staged, was a different matter, and every time I bowled there in the fifties and sixties I found myself wondering how the Middlesex quick bowlers could fail to knock over 150 wickets a season. It had pace, it had bounce; it had everything as far as I was concerned. Len Coldwell, of Worcestershire, making his debut in Tests must have been rather pleased that it was at Lord's. The other debutant, Mickey Stewart, the Surrey opener, probably viewed it with less enthusiasm, especially after seeing what happened to the tourists on the first morning. After winning the toss and deciding to bat they were all out 100, with F.S.T. returning 6 for 31. My second wicket, Burki (who was caught by Ted Dexter) gave me 200 in 47 Tests and I was well pleased.

It had been interesting to watch the development of the newest cricketing nation, for Pakistan had only been admitted to the Test scene at the beginning of the 1950s. They had paid their first visit to England in 1954 and must have wondered what they had let themselves in for because their first Test on English soil did not begin until a quarter to four on the *fourth* day and then, on a rain-affected Lord's wicket, they were bowled out for 87. Not exactly an auspicious start to their first series in England. But before the end of that game, inevitably drawn, a gentleman by the name of Khan Mohammed had clean bowled the great Len Hutton for a duck. The boy wonder, Hanif Mohammed, was not yet into his high-scoring stride but the secret weapon proved to be a big, smiling policeman from Lahore called Fazal Mahmood. He had taken only eight wickets in three Tests when he came to the Oval where he (and Pakistan) completely staggered the English cricket public by taking twelve wickets in the match for 99 and bowling Pakistan to victory by 24 runs.

Fazal was a similar type of bowler to Alec Bedser, a man he greatly admired, so perhaps he was bowling with a sort of psychological boost on Alec's home pitch. What *is* certain is that he enjoyed the experience immensely, so much so that when, twenty-three years later, my collaborator Don Mosey was asked to get an interview 'of about two minutes' with old

Fazal in Karachi, Don began with a straightforward, 'Tell me what you remember about that game at the Oval.' He was keeping half a dozen supplementary questions up his sleeve and a series of detailed notes about that particular Test on a piece of paper in front of him. Forty minutes later, Fazal was still answering the opening question. He'd been right through the details of both England innings, remembered each of the wickets, which ball he had bowled to each batsmen, *why* he had bowled that particualr ball, and all the field placings at the time. It was quite a tour de force and down the line, in the London studio where they had been prepared to record a bit more than the required two minutes, picking out the best bits later, they had run out of tape! The genial Fazal was still big and smiling, and by now a very high-ranking police officer.

So when the 1962 tourists came, we wondered who might be the surprise packet. Hanif, who had seen some palmy days, was now more than a little concerned about bouncers, a matter we quickly worked out and acted upon. Naturally enough, I remember that second Test for my 200th Test wicket and I'm sure a chap called Nasim-ul-Ghani remembers it, too.

Nasim, later to become well-known in the Leagues of the north of England, became the first Pakistani batsman to score a Test hundred in England, after going in as night watchman in their second innings. But what, I wonder, are the memories of that tour cherished by a bowler of medium-paced seamers called Antao D'Souza?

On 16 June he found himself opening the bowling with Mahmood Hussain against Yorkshire at Park Avenue, Bradford. Opening the batting for the home side was a young man playing his first senior match, after scoring 126 not out and 11 not out, 32 and 87 not out, 39 and 104 not out, and 56 in seven innings for the Colts . . . a young man who loved batting. Geoffrey Boycott was his name. In his opening first-class match his record was 'bowled D'Souza 4' in the first innings, 'caught Imtiaz Ahmed bowled D'Souza, 4' in the second. I haven't heard much of Mr D'Souza since that tour but I have often wondered, as Boycott has travelled the world accumulating runs on a vast scale, if Antao, wherever he was, ever nudged his mate in the ribs and said, 'I got that bloke twice in a game for only eight runs, you know.'

12 The Last Gentlemen

Gentlemen v Players – Lord's, 1962

In 1962 the great democratization of cricket took place and the terms 'amateur' and 'professional' left the official vocabulary of the game. On paper we all became simply 'cricketers' and while the old pros felt there might be one or two still lingering about who might more correctly be described as amateurs the situation was no more anachronistic that it had been during the years when we were conscious that quite a number of 'amateurs' were earning more from the game than we were – especially on overseas tours! This meant the end of a very sharply defined distinction in the game and while I welcomed the abolition of such nonsense as 'misters' and separate dressing rooms – indeed, separate gates onto the playing areas in some cases – I was sorry to see the oldest 'one-off' fixture in the game removed from the Lord's calendar: Gentlemen v Players. It was, consequently, a matter of delight to me when I was given command of the mercenaries in the last of the matches which had started the year after the Battle of Trafalgar; nine years before Waterloo.

Thirteen years ago I had come into first-class cricket knowing nothing except how to bowl fast. My years in the game had stimulated a great and abiding affection for it and its traditions, a complete fascination with its roots and its history. It had become to me the greatest game of all and while the distinctions between amateurs and professionals had become blurred around the edges due to the changing economic and social circumstances, the fact that this particular fixture had been played at Lord's since 1806 was enough to make me

I should say Trueman has lost the toss and the Gentlemen have decided to bat first on a plumb wicket.
Roy Ullyett.

cherish it as something which was the very essence of cricket. Once I had become really involved in cricket I wanted to know everything about it and I had spent hours reading books and records to fill my mind with the great deeds of the game. I knew, for instance, that W. G. Grace had played no fewer than 15 three-figure innings in Gentlemen v Players matches and that on his fifty-eighth birthday he hit 74. Over the years there had been more than one such game per season. There was often a 'return' fixture at the Oval, for instance; there were Festival matches, Gents v Players, at places like Scarborough and the Prince's Enclosure at Brighton.

But the real stuff of an amateurs versus professionals encounter must have been in the games played at Lord's. Played there, it had to be right.

In Victorian times, while as many as 200 games would be staged in a season at 'headquarters', few were as important as Gentlemen v Players, except, of course, when a Test match was played there – and we only had Tests against Australia in those days. I have often wondered how I would have managed in the feudal splendour of Victorian cricket.

While I have always been ready to respect authority in its best sense, perhaps I might not have fitted too well into the forelock-touching fraternity which represented professional cricket in the nineteenth century. And then again, I'm not so sure. It's difficult not to relate myself to one E. Peate, a Yorkshire opening bowler who played nine Tests between 1882 and 1896. Peate it was who, in the celebrated Oval match of 1882 (at which the Ashes legend was created) walked to the wicket as last man with nine runs needed for an English victory. He joined *Mr* C. T. Studd, a patrician if ever there was one, in an atmosphere described by the Surrey secretary, C. W. Alcock: 'Men who were noted for their coolness at critical moments were trembling like a leaf. Some were shivering with cold; some even fainted. At times there was an awful silence.'

Now I can identify with that jaunty Yorkshireman, especially when one senses the outrage in a contemporary description of what happened next. 'The Yorkshireman made a hit for two, foolishly tried to repeat it next ball and was clean bowled. When remonstrated with at his foolhardiness in attempting to hit out, Peate had the cool audacity to reply, "I'm very sorry, gentlemen, but the fact is I couldn't trust Mr Studd." This of a batsman who had already played two three-figure innings against the same Australian eleven.' Bloody well said, old Peate. I wouldn't have trusted Mr Studd, either. It was Cromwell, I believe, who had a similar philosophy: 'Give me one russet-coated trooper who knows why he fights and loves what he knows, rather than one who is a gentleman and nothing more.' Quite right, too.

They even interposed their class distinction into the throwing controversy of the 1880s – they had their chuckers and their problems in those days as well. In 1882 a Lancashire fast bowler called Crossland was no-balled out of the game after terrifying the Australians and then bowling out Kent at Maidstone.

'Finally,' according to a contemporary and clearly not entirely disinterested report, 'an umpire was found of resource and courage sufficient to cry "no ball" to each one of Crossland's deliveries with the result that the fast bowler had to be omitted from the county eleven'. So much for the humble North Country pro. It was, apparently, a different matter when Mr Charles Kortright, of Essex, was suspected of an illegal bowling action. Mr Norman Gale immediately sprang to his defence in lyrical fashion, paraphrasing 'Who is Sylvia?' thus:

Who is Kortright, what is he
That Lang doth so commend him?
Bowly, fierce and fast is he
The heavens such pace did lend him
That he might admired be.

Fast is he but is he fair?
For throwing is unkindness.
Those to libel him who dare
Do only prove their blindness
And, being kicked, retract it there.

And yet all bowling gentlemen were not above suspicion and it was the doughty Lord Harris who declined to play for the Gentlemen against the Players in one season because he did not like the action of Mr A. H. Evans and for the same reason he dropped two players from the Kent XI – C. Cooper and Captain Hedley.

The annual fixtures – two of them, at Lord's and the Oval – were usually played during the same week (the first in July) and these were the games that really counted. Others with the same title which were staged at Festivals in September were not really representative of the genuinely gentlemanly playing strength because many of their candidates would be busy on the grouse moors from 12 August onwards. And gradually it was the Lord's fixture which became the real engagement. One of the most exciting was there in 1877 when Mr W. S. Patterson and Fred Grace scored 46 for the last wicket to win even though 'pitted against the flower of professional bowling of that epoch'. In the same game, Mr J. M. Cotterill, of Sussex, hit a seven, a six and three fives!

The professional ranks, while not short of batting strength around this time, were usually much stronger than the opposition in bowling terms so it must have been a bit of a shock to take an eight-wicket hammering in 1882 especially after dismissing the Doctor for only 4; but a record 204 were put together for the third wicket by Charles Studd (of sainted memory) and Lancashire's Alan Steel (Mr, of course).

To honour W. G. on his fiftieth birthday the fixture was played in 1898 on 18 July and the great man marked the occasion with an 'altogether unexpected stand for the tenth partnership with Mr Kortright, who, for seventy long minutes withstood the attack of seven of the best bowlers in England'.

The following season saw the Players total 647 (Abel 197 before he slipped in mid-pitch) Hayward 134 not out and in 1901 it was the professional bowling (Lockwood, Hirst, Trott, Rhodes, Braund and Gunn) which did the trick. At the Oval, however, Mr Ernest Smith hit a ball from the redoubtable

Lohmann into the chimney pots of the pavilion – and that's a big hit in any era. With a 1901 bat it is fantastic.

And so, as I contemplated leading the Players in the last of these fixtures after more than a century and a half, I could look back upon a colourful history which was in many ways the story of first-class cricket itself. I shall not attempt to deny that I was delighted to be asked to take the captaincy. Leading a side at any time is a distinction; to lead one in the final game of a series with a pedigree like Gentlemen v Players, with its century and a half of history, was an honour which gave me very great pleasure indeed.

Yet, to be perfectly frank, the game is not one which conjures up any outstanding memories for me. It ended in a draw . . . a pretty undistinguished draw I seem to recall – at least, not the sort of note on which we would all have liked that series to end. But I do remember the occasion, the honour of the captaincy and one or two incidental matters . . .

The end of the fixture might have been an inevitable consequence of Lord's deciding at last to remove the distinction between amateur and professional players, but the England selectors still took the opportunity (as they had used the fixture in recent years) to look at one or two players they were considering for the next winter's tour. In this case, the tour was the greatest prize of all – to Australia – and one man in particular was under consideration for a place: the Rev. David Sheppard.

From what one could gather, matters had gone a bit beyond the 'consideration' stage because the churches of Australia were apparently preparing for record gates when a touring England cricketer who just happened to be an ordained minister (and one being groomed for stardom, too, if a mixed metaphor is permitted) was likely to be available as a visiting preacher! Well, the Rev. did himself no harm at all in one particular context of the game – a brilliant leg slip catch to dismiss Peter Parfitt. Sheppard was, in fact, a good close fieldsman at the best of times but this was a particularly dazzling effort which sickened my friend (and now neighbour)

Above Watching some slow play in the commentary box at the side of the maestro, John Arlott

Below Always the closest of mates – except in the Roses matches – Brian Statham and myself

Hunte, bowled by Trueman for 18, and Hall, bowled by Trueman for a duck – both in the dramatic third Test against the West Indies at Edgbaston in 1963. The best of the 15,178 balls I bowled in my Test career undoubtedly came in this match

The great Garfield Sobers, who took even the best attack to pieces

An 'out of form' Frank Worrell scored 167 out of the West Indies total of 681-7 in the fourth Test at Trinidad, 1954. Everton Weekes scored 206 and F.S.T. took 1 for 131

Everton de Courcy Weekes, a nice man, a great pal of mine and a magnificent batsman

Wes Hall, a giant of a man, a devastating bowler

Right A truly remarkable man and a great mate of mine, Neil Hawke is down in the record books as my 300th Test victim – N. J. N. Hawke caught Cowdrey bowled Trueman for 14 – England v Australia at the Oval, 1964

Richie Benaud, who was a most intelligent and successful captain – now a colleague of mine on the air

F.S.T. with Ray Lindwall, my hero, and Denis Lillee, Australia's current champion wicket-taker

Left Yorkshire captain Norman Yardley, who bowled me right through the Minor Counties second innings in my Lord's debut – F.S.T. 8 for 70

Keith Miller, one of Australia's finest bowlers, whom I used to pursue in search of useful tips . . .

My Yorkshire colleague Philip Sharpe (batting) and Middlesex captain Peter Parfitt (in the slips) – two of the greatest close catchers of all time

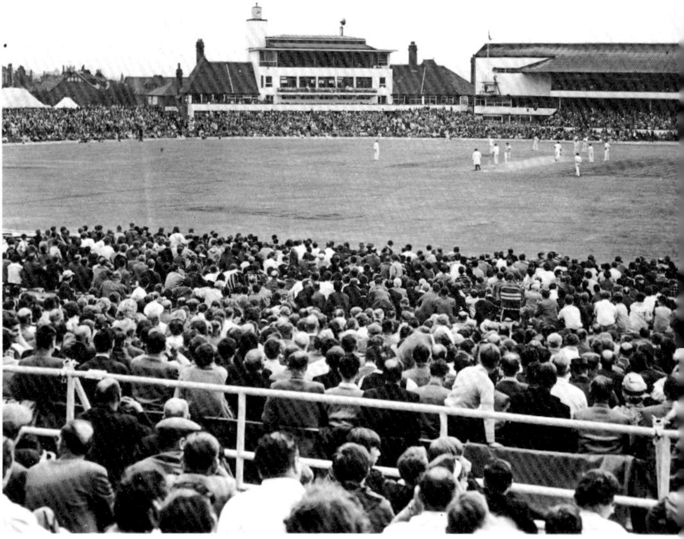

Headingley and Sabina Park – two grounds where the wonderful crowds have sp
me on to some of my greatest performances

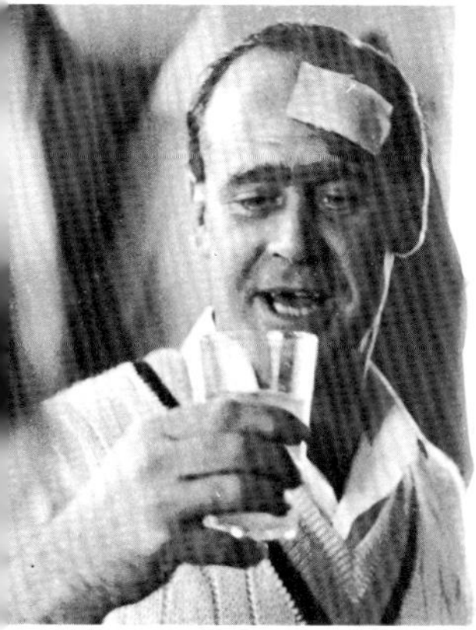

ıbove Brian Close, who walked down the pitch
ɔ play Wes Hall in full cry in the Lord's Test 1963 –
lack and blue, he scored 70 unforgettable runs

ıbove right Len Hutton – every Yorkshire
schoolboy's hero

ight Ken Barrington – a tremendously popular
ıan and a prolific run-maker

elow Basil d'Oliveira – who played some of his
est innings under intense pressure

Bowling in my forties at a slightly slower pace! But every level of cricket has its part to play and every part makes up the whole. The whole is something which may be only a game. But what a game!

P. H. Parfitt. It's a story he delights to tell himself so let him tell it now:

'The score had reached something over 200 for the loss of one wicket and the captain of the Gentlemen, "Lord Edward" Dexter, was reflecting ruefully that the Cambridge University handbook on captaincy contained no particularly relevant advice on situations of that nature. So Dexter decided to put himself on to bowl. He delivered to me the rankest long hop I had seen in a long, long time. I could have hit it anywhere in the ground. It was so rank that I had time to reflect that I *could* reach any far-flung corner of Lords with whatever shot I chose to play. I had also time to reflect that I was a painstakingly coached professional cricketer and as such it would be impolitic of me to use a bad shot to a bad ball.

'So I decided to go by the coaching manual and keep the ball down by a late roll of the wrists and did exactly that – only to see the future Bishop of Liverpool scoop up a blinder of a catch. I stood, gaping my disbelief for a moment, uttering words of self-reproach which were unfit for the ears of a Bootle docker, let alone his spiritual leader, and finally stamped my way back to the pavilion. There I encountered the not-altogether approving gaze of my captain, sitting with his feet on the table and enveloped in smoke from that enormous monstrosity of a pipe: His Majesty, Frederick Sewards Trueman.

'I addressed him, "I'm sorry, captain. I could have hit the bloody thing anywhere. What I was doing to get out, I just don't know." His Majesty removed the pipe and replied with admirable reasonableness, "Don't worry, me old flower. When that chap puts his hands together he's got a better chance than most people in this country." '

That's the Parfitt version and I have no reason to quarrel with it.

The Rev. David made a century in the game as well and so he went to Australia the following winter to the delight of the ecclesiastical fraternity who did, at times, seem to get better attendances than some of the cricket matches.

At the end of the game I took part in a television programme and afterwards set out to drive to Taunton to rejoin Yorkshire, along with Philip Sharpe who had been in the Players side with me at Lord's. Deep in the West Country we took a wrong turning and eventually we arrived at the County Hotel, Taunton, just a little tired.

We booked ourselves early-morning calls; Sharpie got his and I didn't get mine. He made it to the ground on time (although his kit was still in the boot of my car) and I didn't. Vic Wilson, the Yorkshire captain, left me out of the side and informed the press that he had done so. I arrived at the ground half an hour late, but still half an hour before the scheduled start of play, to find myself ordered home to Yorkshire. It was a sour and bitter occasion. The only man to get any pleasure out of it was, I think, Peter Wight, the Guyanese batsman who used to get 2000 runs a season regularly but none of them against Yorkshire. I had just a slight psychological advantage over P. B. Wight when we played against each other. On this occasion he scored 215.

My travelling companion from Lord's to Taunton has his own memory of that final Gentlemen v Players match. Sharpie had a great season in 1962 and an even better one in 1963 when he won his first Test cap against the West Indies. He has always wondered if he might have been called up earlier – to make that tour of Australia and New Zealand *instead of* David Sheppard – if an edge from the Rev. early in his big innings had carried just a couple of feet more. If it had, you can be sure the little feller would have held it. I would have been happy to take him round with me forever, just to take slip catches. And if that one had carried it is not inconceivable that *he* would have gone to Australia in place of the future bishop. But then Sharpie might not have filled the churches quite so well as David did.

13 The Close Encounter

Gloucestershire v Yorkshire – Bristol, 1962

Now for a game in which I didn't take part (or rather one or two games, all in the same city) but which is a part of Yorkshire folklore.

I am not quite sure what it is about Bristol that seems to bring out the worst of Yorkshire cricket. It's a lovely city, the county ground is a good one, there are a lot of good golf courses around (and that used to be important when we played two three-day championship matches a week and Sunday, mercifully, was a day of rest) and there was always a good social life there.

The Berni steakhouses were starting to spread around the country but in the fifties and even the early sixties it still wasn't easy to find a good steak in every eating house. So fixtures at Bristol, with a Berni steakhouse, ought to have been popular. There was the sherry, too, available by the schooner in any one of those marvellous wine bars and cellars. Maybe that was the trouble. The sherry. Certainly it had a lot to do with one spectacular defeat we suffered there – and in the season when we finally won the championship again after years in the wilderness, 1959.

It was the Rummer Bar that did it – a famous hostelry right in the city centre and dangerously close to our hotel. There the sherry flowed freely in the stone-walled cellars and some of the younger Yorkshire players hadn't the sense to realize that sherry is all very well when drunk gently and reverently as a pleasant apéritif, but is something entirely different when flung down like a half-pint of Tetley's bitter.

We were two games away from the end of the season and while we had done well under the captaincy of Ronnie Burnet the title didn't seem quite possible as we went to Bristol on 22 August after a defeat at Bath. (Little did we realize that after winning the penultimate game of the season at Worcester we were to go to Hove to finish in such a blaze of glory as the county had not seen for a very long time.)

We lost the toss at Bristol, spent the whole of the first day in the field and saw Gloucestershire declare at 294 for 8. I say 'we' because any Yorkshire player of my day instinctively thought like that. As a matter of fact I wasn't playing in that game, otherwise I might have had something to say about what went on, but this is just one example of the effect Bristol seemed to have on the Yorkshire team. For some reason they have never been able to explain, some of the younger end started on the sherry after that first day's play and, as usual, it slipped down so smoothly that they didn't realize just how potent it is in bulk.

Not until chucking-out time, that is, when they had to start the walk back to the hotel. The Royal Hotel, where the team was staying, is a very short distance away from the Rummer Bar – but not if your legs have gone. A couple of now-distinguished figures in the game might blush to be reminded of that night but . . . serve 'em right. They were young and foolish in 1959. Don Wilson, now head coach at Lord's, was making his way as a slow left-armer in the Yorkshire side and Jackie Birkenshaw, today an elder statesman with Worcestershire, got into the team occasionally when Raymond Illingworth was not available to do the off spinning. 'Wils' found those long, spindly legs wouldn't work at all after a lavish infusion of Bristol Cream and he crawled from the bar to the hotel on his hands and knees without any recollection of that rather eccentric trip. The following morning he woke up feeling like death and discovered that the knees of his smart new suit had been replaced by holes. His next discovery was that his roommate, one J. Birkenshaw, had apparently spent the night on his knees too, but with his head in the washbasin, and there he was, still quite unconscious, as Don surveyed the tattered remnants of twenty-five quid spent at Montague Burton's. Once they had tottered to the ground it soon became clear that they had not been alone in their revelries because Yorkshire were bowled out for 35 by those two medium-fast masters of seam bowling – Tony Brown (7 for 11) and David Smith (3 for 16). Only Brian Bolus, with 12 not out going in at number five, reached double figures, and when Yorkshire followed on and were shot out for 182, exactly half that total came from the bat of the sober and righteous J. B. Bolus. We were beaten by an innings and 77 runs inside two days.

Four years later, in 1963, there was another social gathering in Bristol. Brian Close was now captain of Yorkshire but while the county were in Gloucestershire he and I were playing against the West Indies at Lord's. Ray Illingworth was injured so Jimmy Binks was the county captain. In those days the Yorkshire team were accompanied around the cricket circuit by their personal press entourage . . . cricket-writers from six Yorkshire papers and four 'nationals'. We had a bit of popular appeal in those days. Naturally enough, virtually living together for four months a year, players and press were pretty close and a lot of friendships began in those days which have endured. And, I suppose, we were a rather convivial band of brothers.

It didn't really take much for a party to get started in the evenings especially, as on this occasion, when rain had meant a lot of frustrating hours during the day sitting around doing nothing very much. So on the second night of the Bristol game a noisy party started in the hotel – not the Royal but a smaller place up in Clifton where they were not quite so used to singing parties at eleven o'clock at night. So loud was the singing as midnight approached that it woke a fair cross-section of the residents of the zoo, a couple of hundred yards away. And with lions, hyenas and baboons in the nocturnal chorus a major part of the sedate suburb of Clifton spent a largely sleepless night.

Not unnaturally a violent letter of complaint was dispatched next morning from the hotel management to the Yorkshire headquarters in Leeds.

Meanwhile, back at Lord's, Closey and I were involved in what Wisden described as 'one of the most dramatic Test matches ever played in England'. Remember it? Do you remember Closey walking down the pitch to meet Wes Hall in full cry and Big Wes collapsing in a heap because he couldn't believe it? Closey was black and blue after taking Hall and Griffiths on the chest (and sometimes on the chin) and he scored 70 runs. Do you remember Colin Cowdrey getting a whole series of short ones from Hall and Griffith and eventually having to retire with a broken bone above the left wrist? And do you remember how he came out again as last man with six runs needed and two balls to be bowled, intending to bat left-handed if he had to take strike? He didn't, as it happened. David Allen played out the last two and the game was drawn, but you would think that enough had happened for people to remember the game clearly enough and those who had taken part. Even allowing for the agonizing last few overs you might think people would remember someone who had taken 11 West Indian wickets for 152 in the match. Never take such things for granted, especially in Yorkshire.

Returning to the county side from the Test, not expecting to be hailed as a hero (you'd really have to take all 20 wickets and get a ton as well to impress Yorkshiremen), but expecting that someone might just mention the Test in passing, I found myself summoned to a committee meeting. And there, larger than life as always, was Brian Sellers, our chairman.

A. B. Sellers. The Crackerjack. The martinet who ruled his superb 1930s side with a cast-iron rod reinforced with concrete. The man who called spades bloody shovels in any gathering, no matter how august. Dear old Brian Sellers, but I didn't feel quite so affectionately disposed towards him at that moment.

'Now then, Trueman,' he bellowed, brandishing what I had no means of knowing was the complaint from a Bristol hotel, 'you've been at it again. What the blue blazes do you mean by letting the young lads create merry hell down in Bristol? When you're the captain you're supposed to look after them, not let them run riot and turn bloody hotels upside down.'

I was just a bit taken aback. 'At Bristol, you say?' I queried.

'Yes, Bristol. Don't look so bloody surprised. You were in charge, weren't you? Closey was playing in the Test match.'

It was not the moment for subtlety. 'I am sorry, Mr Chairman, that it has escaped your notice that *I* was in that match as well. And if you look it up you might find I took a wicket or two. Good morning.' And back I went to being just another Yorkshire player.

We move back now to Bristol, 1962, and once again I was not on parade (Gloucestershire v Yorkshire coincided with England v Pakistan at Trent Bridge). Amongst the Brylcreem awards for outstanding performances at that time was one for the highest number of catches taken by a fieldsman during the season. In fierce contention for the prize were two Yorkshiremen, D. B. Close and P. J. Sharpe, two of the greatest close-catchers of all time. While Philip Sharpe remained posted at slip – his concentration as absolute when the last ball of the day was being bowled as it was for the first – Closey was used by the skipper Vic Wilson in a whole variety of positions . . . slip, silly point, lunatic short leg. Indeed, Closey would have stood in the crease with the batsman if the laws had allowed it. Gloucestershire faced a first-innings total of 230 and the pitch looked ready to take spin. Six overs of Tony Nicholson and Mel Ryan to take the shine off, and the spinners were in action. Closey was posted in Ray Illingworth's leg-trap, breathing down the neck of Martin Young. Young decided to do something about this, swung to leg and off the meat of the bat the ball struck Closey squarely in the middle of that lofty brow.

While everyone stood in horror, waiting for the Incredible Hulk to drop dead with a fractured skull, he stood there watching the ball as it ballooned in a gentle arc to Sharpie at first slip. More by reflex action than anything else Philip caught it but remained open-mouthed, staring at Closey. He need have expected nothing else than the remark which followed.

'You're not getting *all* the credit for that, Sharpie,' said the Hulk. 'I'm claiming half the catch.' And he did.

Closey is, of course, indestructible. Playing golf in a

Celebrity Pro-Am tournament at the Cambridgeshire Hotel he was doing rather well after the first four holes and, as usual, got a bit wrapped up in his own game so that after putting his tee-shot into light rough at the fifth he forgot his partners for a moment and strolled on, anxious to make sure of his own lie. He didn't notice that one of the four was playing his second shot as he browsed around in the grass at the edge of the fairway – until the partner's ball struck him squarely on the back of the head. Most people would have been felled by such a blow. Not D. B. Close. As he told the story in the clubhouse afterwards one of his audience, horrified, asked, 'What on earth happened to you?'

Closey, with a snort of righteous indignation, replied, 'I dropped four bloody shots in the next three holes.'

It was this sort of Brian Close anecdote, told by us to Radio 3 listeners on Test Match Special, which led a listener in Lancashire to ask if Brian was descended from the Vikings. His question was prompted, he said, by one of the sagas which told how one of the legendary heroes took off his helmet in battle because of the heat and was struck a whole series of blows on his bald head with swords and axes. Not one of them caused a wound 'but sparks flew at each blow'.

There can be no doubt at all. It *was* one of Closey's ancestors.

14 The New Record

New Zealand v England – Christchurch, 1963

Lancaster Park, Christchurch, in New Zealand has a lot of memories for sportsmen of two games – rugby union and cricket. Primarily it is a rugby ground, as are three of the other New Zealand Test stadiums, Carisbrooke in Dunedin, Eden Park (Auckland) and the ground at Napier which was used for Tests while the Basin Reserve in Wellington (a soccer ground, this one) was being rebuilt in 1979–80.

It is not always easy to get the real feeling of Test cricket on a ground which has been built specifically for a winter game. There is not the essential charm of cricket grounds; it seems more utilitarian than aesthetically pleasing. If you look over the stands and beyond the boundaries of Lancaster Park in one direction you have an entirely pleasant view of the Port Hills, but if you allow the eye to wander 45 degrees to the right it comes to rest on as hideous a gasworks as you will encounter in Rotherham or Widnes.

Christchurch is, nevertheless, a pleasant place to rest a touring head for a week or two. It is described as the most 'English' of New Zealand cities with its famous public school and university, its standing as the cultural centre of New Zealand, and the attractive little River Avon winding its way through the flower-filled suburbs. I like Christchurch, just as I like the rest of the New Zealand I have seen as a player or, some years later, on a speaking tour. The people are friendly and hospitable in the extreme. Basically they are as reserved as their Australian neighbours are boisterous, but make a friend of a Kiwi and you have made a friend for life.

So I have several reasons for having pleasant memories of New Zealand and a particular one for recalling my 1963 visit to Christchurch with special affection. It was there, on 15 March, that I overtook Brian Statham's record of 242 Test wickets and when the game ended four days later I had taken my 250th in my fifty-sixth Test.

But the story really begins a couple of months earlier at the Adelaide Oval in South Australia; the fourth Test of the tour which saw the Rev. D. S. Sheppard filling the churches, even if our 1–1 Test series with three draws did not fill the Test arenas. The first was a high-scoring draw at Woolloongabba, Brisbane. We won the second, in Melbourne, where Sheppard scored 113 in our eight-wickets victory.

In Sydney, Australia levelled the series, also by eight wickets after we had been bowled out for 104 in the second innings leaving my mate 'George' Statham and myself only 67 to bowl at. We dismissed Bill Lawry and Neil Harvey before they got the runs but in a batting line-up which included Bobby Simpson, Brian Booth and Norm O'Neill (Richie Benaud at number nine!) it was an impossible job. So we went to the beautiful Adelaide Oval all square and this, and the final Test, were drawn – but not before a bit of history had been made.

Now David Sheppard naturally enough attracted a lot of attention, and his ministerial status made him the target for a certain amount of ripe Australian wit. Neil Hawke, who made his Test debut in the fifth (Sydney) Test, recalls with delight the raucous, solitary voice from the Hill when Alan Davidson bowled a whole over to the Rev. which he was able to ignore completely: 'Carm orn, Dyvo – lead 'im into temptyshun.'

George figures in a nice one, too. Sheppard was having a rather tough morning fielding in the deep. Some of his returns were a bit wayward, as the commentators say today, and his hands were not quite as safe, out in the deep, as they had been when disposing of Peter Parfitt in the Gentlemen v Players match at Lord's six months earlier. Finally he caught a steepler and in a positive paroxysm of delight, hurled the ball high in the air. As he waited for it to come down his ecstasy was chastened by a plaintive cry from the bowler, J. B. Statham, which could be heard all over the ground: 'Come on, Rev. It was a no ball and they've run three already!' But the Rev. smiled his way engagingly through it all – and got some runs, too.

However, in the fourth Test at Adelaide, Statham the bowler was a bit surprised to see Sheppard at short leg and me stationed at long leg and asked the captain, Ted Dexter, the reason for this. George was more than a little surprised to be told that it was because I had a good arm and some of the fielders had difficulty in getting their throws back to the wicket-keeper from the boundary edge. Now this is far from unknown in Australia where some of the grounds are immense. There are quite a few Test fieldsmen around who will tell you of the problems they have encountered in making long returns at Melbourne in particular where the boundary ropes sometimes seem miles away. Anyway, George didn't think much of his mate being posted a hundred yards away from the bat. He wanted me in close.

So after a bit of discussion I was brought up to a close-catching position, either third slip or second gulley. Statham bowled a couple and then got one to bounce and leave a left-handed batsman, Barrie Shepherd, and I took the catch. It was a moment to savour because that was George's 237th Test wicket and it took him past Alec Bedser's record.

I was delighted to be the catcher because George and I were great friends throughout our Test careers – indeed our whole cricketing lives – and we didn't need too much persuading to break out the champagne that night. There was another cause for celebration in the course of that game because another of my very good friends, Ken Barrington, hit 132 not out in our second innings and we could well have won the Test but for rain in the middle of it. Kenny reached his 100 with a six and some years later that indefatigable researcher Bill Frindall came up with the discovery that this was the first time that had been done in an Australia–England series since Joe Darling in 1897–8. No wonder cricket is a statistician's delight! But let's get back to the point . . .

In that match I overtook Alec Bedser's 237 as well; Brian Statham took his total to 242 in the fourth and fifth Tests and then opted to return home rather than go on to New Zealand for the final month of the tour. This used to happen quite a bit in the days when New Zealand only received a visit from an MCC side at the end of a strenuous three months or so in Australia. Many players were tired; some wanted to get back to their families; as a result New Zealand missed seeing a lot of Test cricketers I am sure they would have liked to see. They missed seeing Brian Statham on that occasion and the fast-bowling complement for the three Tests across the Tasman Sea was David Larter, Barry Knight, Len Coldwell and myself. The records started going down (or being chalked up) as soon as we went into Test action because in the first, at Eden Park, England's 562 for 7 declared was then the highest against New Zealand. Kenny Barrington hit a marvellous 126 and then Parfitt and Knight had a record sixth-wicket partnership of 240. We won by an innings and 215. At Wellington, I nipped five wickets to put me one behind my old mate on 241 Test victims, but before we went on to Christchurch there was another bit of record-breaking – a ninth-wicket partnership of 163 between Colin Cowdrey and Alan Smith, nice one for Oxford University!

Barrington, following up his hundred in Auckland with 76 at Wellington, had 1 for 1 in the New Zealand first innings and 3 for 32 in the second with his leg-spinners and googlies. Kenny was a tremendously popular man with New Zealand cricket crowds so it was no surprise to learn of the great success of his tour as manager in 1978. In Dunedin on that tour he endeared himself to a future generation of players and spectators by lining up the youngsters one lunchtime during the match against Otago and having them bowl to him with a half-dollar piece on top of the stumps instead of bails. Anyone who dislodged the coin kept it and quite a few lads went back to their seats fifty cents better off. Ken could play down the *wrong* line when he wanted!

Back to Christchurch. The crowd knew the situation and

when I had Bill Playle caught by Barrington it was possible to sense the air of expectancy in Lancaster Park. And, of course, the inevitable happened. Could I get the next wicket? Could I heck . . . not until another 80 runs had been added by Graham Dowling and Barry Sinclair. It always seems that you beat the bat more without getting nick, that the batsman plays and misses twice as much, when you want a wicket very, very badly. And I wanted one now – very badly indeed. I think the crowd wanted it as well. Next to a New Zealand century, or that elusive first win over the old country, I think they would have been happy enough to settle for a record set up before their eyes. I tried just about every kind of delivery in the repertoire but if they got an edge it didn't go to hand and if they didn't get an edge it would shave the stumps. I had just about given up hope of getting one of those two and was beginning to think I might have to settle for someone else breaking the partnership when I dropped one short to Sinclair. He went back to pull me – and stepped on his wicket. That was number 243 on my scalp belt and I was a very happy feller.

By way of celebration, it seemed, the wickets now came without further trouble – 2 for 16 in the first innings, 7 for 75 in the second and by now I was up to the 250 mark. It was a really good feeling. Amongst the first to offer congratulations were Lord Nugent, President of MCC, and the Duke of Norfolk, who was the tour manager – pretty close to a royal reception. Then the telegrams started to come in from various county clubs in England, from cricket lovers all over the country and my native county, from MCC at Lord's, from show business personalities, from individual players, and from other cricket-playing countries. But officially from the Yorkshire County Cricket Club – nothing. I was surprised and, I don't mind admitting it, I was hurt, too. Everyone in the world of cricket, it seemed, recognized that some sort of milestone had been reached except the officials of the club for which I played. I am *still* waiting for Yorkshire's congratulations.

When I got back to England, the county president, Sir William Worsley – incidentally, one of the greatest gentlemen I

A robot bowler is invented

ever met in the game – offered his congratulations when we met at the pre-season lunch where the players traditionally get together with county officials. Sir William said, 'I'm sorry I was not there to see it, Freddie, but I was in Hong Kong, visiting my daughter.'

I could not resist replying, 'Yes, sir. I know where you were. That is apparently the reason why I received no congratulations from my own county.'

He stared at me. 'What do you mean?' I explained that I had had some acknowledgement from just about everyone in cricket except Yorkshire CCC. He could not believe it. I believed he thought it was a joke in bad taste but I assured him that no telegram had been sent by my county. 'Why?' he asked incredulously.

'Well,' I said, 'I can only assume it was *because* you were in Hong Kong. I mentioned the matter to the county secretary, John Nash, and he said no telegram could be sent because the president was out of the country. I could only assume, Sir William, that no telegrams of congratulation were sent out from headquarters unless the president was there to pay for them!'

Fortunately there is always another side to a story like that. Within a matter of about forty-eight hours of my beating the record we were all at the dinner given by the New Zealand Board of Control. During the speeches, the New Zealand captain, John Reid, suddenly produced the ball I had been using when the 243rd wicket was taken. It had been mounted and inscribed in a matter of hours and there and then John presented it to me. It is one of a nice little collection I keep in a showcase at home and I sometimes look at it with a bit of a smile – not so much for its special significance as for the fact that a landmark was reached with a 'hit-wicket'.

Out of 307 Test victims, I only had three hit-wickets: Barrie Sinclair was the third and last. The first – also in New Zealand – was S. N. McGregor during the second Test in Auckland in 1959, and at Old Trafford in 1961 Norm O'Neill became number two.

When I had the pleasure of going back to New Zealand in the early seventies to give a series of talks I was able to do the sightseeing that there never seems to be time to indulge in when you are touring. I remember the wonderful beauty spots of South Island, especially Queenstown where 7000-foot mountains look down on lakes of fabulous blue.

However, Barry Sinclair provides my personal memory of Lancaster Park, Christchurch. Fifteen years later Ian Botham was to score his first Test century on the same ground and I'm sure it will figure pretty prominently when he looks back over his Test career. And, from that same Test, I wonder how Ewen Chatfield looks back on his running out of Derek Randall – the non-striker backing up too far as Chatfield ran in to bowl? I wonder if, with hindsight, he would still do it?

15 The First Ton

Northamptonshire v Yorkshire – Northampton, 1963

Scratch the surface of a bowler – *any* bowler, really, but certainly every *fast* bowler who ever lived – and you'll find a frustrated batsman. Sometimes he is not entirely frustrated, because just occasionally the batsman in him escapes to leave his mark on the game. And if the escape finds its way into the record books, you can bet your bottom dollar that your bowler will regard that record as the one he always wants to look at first when the pages are turned.

Take Alec Bedser, for instance: a magnificent bowler, with 236 Test wickets to his name and afterwards chairman of the England selectors for many years. But the way to bring a smile of happy nostalgia to Big Al's face is to remind him, not of any of his outstanding bowling returns, or his great duels with Australians like Arthur Morris, but of an innings in the fourth Test against Australia at Headingley in 1948: A. V. Bedser, c and b Johnson, 79. It was one of those situations non-batsmen love: to go in as night watchman and show the so-called front-line batsmen how it should be done, but in Alec's case this was not a moment of crisis in the last half hour. The score was in fact 268 for 2 when he went to the wicket. England finally totalled 496, then scored 365 for 8 declared in their second innings – and still lost – so you may gather that it was a pitch more calculated to delight the eye of a batsman than a bowler.

Jim Laker recalls it with no affection at all but his Surrey team-mate will always have a soft spot in his heart for that particular Headingley wicket. His 79 runs were achieved on the first and second days, and over the weekend he visited the market town of Skipton, which was the home of the Headingley groundsman, Percy Moulton.

With that fierce pride in *any* local personality and contempt for outsiders, no matter how distinguished, which characterizes most Yorkshiremen, one of the drinkers in a pub where Alec called for a spot of refreshment asked him, 'What's ter think o' that pitch at Headingley, then?'

Alec had just spent all Saturday bowling on it and, just for the moment, the delights of his 79 runs had receded to the back of his mind. So, not unnaturally, his reply was, 'Not much.' This was taken as a grievous personal insult by the 'townie' of Percy Moulton.

He came back swiftly and with ponderous sarcasm, 'It can't be so bad if *thar* can get runs on it.' Even in your finest hour, you can't win!

In pre-war years there was always a buzz of expectancy audible in any ground when Big Jim Smith, of Middlesex, or Arthur Wellard, of Somerset, walked to the wicket. These were men who not only delighted in batting but they could also be relied upon for some spectacular hitting as well. After the war the tradition was carried on by such bowlers as Ellis Robinson and Johnny Wardle, in Yorkshire; by Dick Pollard, of Lancashire; Tom Pritchard and Charlie Grove, of Warwickshire, and a handful of others scattered around the seventeen counties. But in the sixties and seventies, a combination of covered wickets, changes in the lbw laws and delusions of grandeur on the part of some bowlers produced the forward lunge, bat and pad together.

The result of all this was that the game was held up for no particular purpose, the opposition was frustrated and the spectators were bored. That is one of the reasons why the arrival, in the late seventies, of a player like Ian Botham was such a tonic to those who paid to be entertained. Botham arrived, of course, as a genuine all-rounder – far from being a quick bowler who simply struck the ball vigorously. But it was a marvellous boost for the game to find a man whose clean striking of the ball was carried out with the same sense of joy as the out-and-out tonkers of old.

In my day it was rare enough to find a nine-ten-jack who could bat at all and rarer still to find one willing to chance his arm by attempting a few lusty blows. That is why I think Yorkshire, with Don Wilson and myself in the lower orders, seemed to contribute something extra in entertainment value. I *liked* to bat – no I *loved* it – but as a strike-bowler I didn't like my runs to take up too much time because quite apart from the fact that my natural instinct was to get the ball in my hand and start bowling, I wanted to be as fresh and rested as possible for that part of the fray.

Gradually, from being the rawest number eleven in the business, I began to develop a batting technique. You can't spend around 75 per cent of your life bowling to great batsmen without observing them closely. In looking for their weaknesses you inevitably learn to appreciate their strengths . . . you don't try bouncers to this fellow, you make sure that one is kept on the front foot, so-and-so is a bit dodgy around the off stump, what's-his-name doesn't like the leg-stump yorker. You *learn*, all the time.

By the early sixties I had more than a decade of experience stored up in my mental card-index system and from time to time I would try out a shot which was the speciality of some top-class batsman I had recently been trying to dismiss. Of course people expected to see most of my runs gathered in the area between mid-wicket and long on and if anyone pitched up a half-volley I was happy to oblige. But the classic cover drive was not unknown to the Trueman bat, and slowly more and more people began to tell me that I ought to score more runs than I did. Herbert Sutcliffe was one of these, and I thought that if a great batsman like that could fancy me to score runs it ought to be possible. Sir William Worsley, the Yorkshire president, made the same point, backed up by a promise that when I scored my first century, a cheque would go into the post the same day! All the same, it's not easy to get hundreds when you regularly bat at number eight or nine. I remember young David

Smith ('D.H.K.', now resident in South Africa) getting trials with Derbyshire and going on one of their pre-season practice matches to play in Cheshire. Before the match he dashed out of the pavilion excitedly to tell a friend who had come to wish him well, 'The skipper says that if I get a hundred today there will be a first-team chance for me.' And back he went into the dressing room, his heart brimming with hope, to see his name at number nine in the batting order. They have never been renowned for taking unnecessary risks in Derbyshire!

So I had had my fifties and sixties and they had delighted me. Expert judges had said I *ought* to get a hundred; I *wanted* to get a hundred; it only remained for the opportunity to arrive. It arrived on Saturday, 4 May 1963, at Northampton. Brian Close had taken over the county captaincy that season and two of the traditional opening matches – against MCC at Lord's and Cambridge University at Fenners – had been drawn. This was his first County Championship match as captain and naturally enough he wanted to do well. Instead, he found himself surrounded by the ruins of an innings in the first couple of hours: Stott out for 4, Sharpe 4, Padgett 18, Illingworth 10, the up-and-coming Boycott 10. Despite the fact that Closey himself was going like a bomb we were 106 for 5 and the next man in was F. S. Trueman.

Ken Taylor was out of our side and Closey had said to me before we batted, 'I'm sorry, F.S., but you'll have to bat number seven.'

Perhaps, subconsciously, I was thinking my chance had come at last, but I doubt it. Certainly, I was not worried about promotion in the order and I expect I made that clear by replying, 'That's all right. I'll do my best.'

'You'll *have* to,' said the captain, a trifle grimly. Technical matters of that nature have always been discussed in the Yorkshire dressing room with the same graciousness . . . 'We don't play this game for fun . . .'

So there we were, five down against a Northamptonshire attack that wasn't the best in the world, as I joined my captain: a rather worried captain, but being Closey, he was worried only about getting somebody to stay with him. He was going *really* well, showing all that immense talent with the bat which he showed us too rarely. *He* had no fears or doubts at all – except for the bloke at the other end. Well, he didn't have to worry about my end for a bit.

There was always an odd sort of rivalry between Closey and me. I think he believed at times that he could use the new ball better then me and there were certainly other times when I have been sure that blindfold I could bat better than him. This wasn't one of those days. The old lad was going like an absolute bomb and I wasn't doing too badly myself. I reached 50 and we were now well past the 200 mark. Then I played a loose shot to Ollie Milburn and – incredibly – that prince of wicketkeepers, Keith Andrew, put down the catch. Before I had time to draw my next relieved breath, Closey was down the pitch to me, 'Come on, get your head down; we still need a lot of runs.'

Some people are never bloody well satisfied. I ground my teeth and thought, 'You beauty, Closey. What the hell do I have to do to impress you?' So I *got* my head down. From 106 for 5, we reached a total of 339 all out. Closey and I added 166 for the eighth wicket; he got 161 and I hit 104 . . . my first ton. That was on Saturday. The following Monday Sir William Worsley's cheque for £10 was waiting for me.

They do say that these things are infectious and in my penultimate game of that season I reached 100 for the second time, this time exactly 100 and it was not out. This is the innings (mentioned elsewhere in these reminiscences) on which you might win yourself a few bob: Q. Did Freddie Trueman ever hit a century for England? A. Yes, at Scarborough on 4 September 1963, England v Young England in the Festival. And this was batting at number nine!

But there were no worries for me about running out of partners because the man at the other end when I went in to bat was the Barnacle himself, now my Test Match Special radio colleague and good friend, Trevor Bailey. I don't know how many he had scored when I went in, but he was 44 not out when we declared and he had already had a pretty fair stand with

David Allen. But of course Trevor wasn't bothered about *his* score and once I had got going he played the game in the best Festival tradition. I've always got on well with the crowds at Scarborough and as they started to enjoy the stand more and more, Trevor pushed the singles expertly to give me the regular strike, with the result that of our unbeaten partnership of 120, I scored 100. As a combination of stroke-play and grafter, I reckon Trevor Bailey and Freddie Trueman were pretty useful!

I can't honestly claim that the Festival innings had the same intrinsic value as the one at Northampton, but in terms of artistic interpretation it might have got higher marks from the judges. Perhaps not from Richard Hutton, though. He took the second new ball for Young England and with a fine touch of lese-majesty let me have a bouncer. I tried to hook – not a stroke at which I was especially adept – got a top edge and the ball dropped just short of a six over the top of the wicketkeeper. 'Archie' Hutton delivered himself of an unsolicited testimonial which might not have pleased the school chaplain at Repton but which had both Trevor and myself doubled up with laughter. And when the partnership was over, Roger Prideaux, the Northamptonshire skipper who was leading Young England at Scarborough, somewhat reproachfully inquired, 'Why d'you always pick on me, Fred?'

My hat trick of hundreds had to wait almost two years and, to my delight, it came, once again, at Scarborough. One month earlier I had played my sixty-seventh, and what turned out to be my last, Test match, against the New Zealanders at Lord's. Whether or not I sensed that my Test career had ended, I don't know. Perhaps I did realize that it was going to be difficult to come back, at least as a number one strike bowler, at the age of thirty-four but I was still nursing thoughts of being able to run through sides with my cutters when conditions were right. And my batting was 'coming on', as they say. I started out with my usual quicker stuff against Middlesex at Scarborough on 21 July 1965, and got nowhere at all during the morning session.

At lunch Middlesex were over a hundred with only one wicket down and I sat in the dressing room brooding darkly while the others were eating upstairs. Had I really lost all my zip? I didn't think so – I would never allow myself to think so. But . . . not a single wicket in the morning spell, and at Scarborough, too. My friends there expected something better of F.S.T. at North Marine Road and I yearned to give it to them. But what was the matter? Middlesex weren't all *that* good; Eric Russell and Peter Parfitt, later to become a great mate, not out at lunch with over a hundred on the board. It just wasn't right. The others trooped back from lunch, we took the field, and after a couple of overs Closey said to me, 'Come on now, F.S., it's moving about all over the place. Get stuck into 'em.'

'Moving about?' I snarled, incredulously. 'Moving *about*? That's why they're a hundred-and-odd for one, is it?'

Jimmy Binks joined the debate. 'I tell you, Fred. It's really moving. Come on, knock 'em over.'

Still a bit sceptical, I took the ball, came in from the full run, and suddenly it all came right. J. T. Murray, the great trouper and a central figure in the Middlesex chat squad, bowled for nought; J. M. Brearley, a promising young batsman from Cambridge University, bowled for nought; Ron Hooker, a fine county all-rounder, bowled for nought, followed by John Price and Bob White. I had taken 5 for none, all clean bowled, and Middlesex were all out 150. That restored my bowling pride for that day; sweet success smiled tenderly upon me on the Thursday as well. We were 207 for 7; I went in at number nine – 57 runs on. Not exactly a position of prosperity but not entirely a crisis, either. Peter Chadwick, a talented batsman who afterwards went to Derbyshire, was at the other end, an uncapped player but a good one. Together we put on 147 and I was 101 when I sent a fierce return catch to 'Knocker' White. It nearly took him back to the boundary but he held on. Ted Lester, our scorer, came into the dressing room between the innings and grinned at me, 'You're supposed to take a new guard and carry on once you've reached a hundred, Fred . . . now you're an established century-maker.'

16 The Vintage Year

Yorkshire v West Indies – Middlesbrough, 1963

Yorkshire started to play county matches at Middlesbrough in 1956 and the move was an immediate success. Apart from the enthusiasm of cricketers born on the south side of the River Tees there is tremendous support for the game in the two minor counties north of it – Durham and Northumberland – and they quickly showed that they were keen enough to make a round trip of well over a hundred miles in some cases to watch first-class games.

One of the keenest followers during those early days on the newest Yorkshire ground was a young man playing centre forward for Middlesbrough Football Club – Brian Clough. Don Wilson, later to become head coach at Lord's, remembers the Acklam Park ground with affection as the one where he registered a hat trick against Nottinghamshire in 1959. Brian Bolus, who left Yorkshire to captain both Nottinghamshire and Derbyshire in the sixties, will recall returning 'home' to carry his bat through the Nottinghamshire Gillette Cup innings in 1963 at Acklam Park for 100. And I'm pretty sure Butch White will always remember his 6-for-10 performance there in 1965 when Hampshire bowled us out for 23!

Two years before that, during the West Indies tour of 1963, cricket was well established on Teesside and the support had been so good that the county committee paid Middlesbrough the compliment of staging a match against the tourists there. It was a major sporting occasion because not only does the cricket club share the park with Middlesbrough Rugby Club but two of the great supporters of cricket occasions there were the

Thomas brothers, Harold and Eric, who were directors of Middlesbrough *Football* Club. For the West Indies visit the local organizing committee had pulled out all the stops and there was a sort of Festival atmosphere with marquees erected around the rugby end of the ground. There was, however, nothing of the light-hearted Festival atmosphere about the cricket. Star players didn't take a rest during tourist matches in those days . . . oh no! Everyone wanted to play, even if it meant throwing away a pair of crutches and claiming that a broken leg had miraculously healed. And in Yorkshire, everyone wanted to be involved in *beating* the tourists because nothing less than victory was contemplated.

In batting strength, the West Indies were nothing if not formidable with that fine captain Frankie Worrell opening with Joey Carew. They were followed by Rohan Kanhai, then at the height of his power, Seymour Nurse and the great Garfield Sobers, then Basil Butcher and at number seven, Joe Solomon . . . a pretty impressive line-up. And spearheading their bowling was one Charles Griffith.

Now I'd seen Charlie in the West Indies but this bowler bore no resemblance to the one I'd watched on the other side of the Atlantic. C. Griffith was now about two and a half times as quick off a run which was four times as long. In one innings he sent Jackie Hampshire to hospital, in the other Doug Padgett. He was quick, and unpredictably quick at times, leading to grave suspicions about the legality of his action, especially when he bowled the yorker or the bouncer. We totalled 226 which, in all the circumstances, was a respectable total, with Bryan Stott making 65 batting at number six and yours truly hitting 55 at number eight.

That year, 1963, was a vintage year for Trueman the bat because just under four months later I made that maiden hundred for England at Scarborough against Young England. And that was just as sweet as 55 against the tourists before I was caught behind off Griffith. It wasn't a big total, but the wicket was doing a bit and it gave us something to bowl at.

My current opening partner was Mel Ryan. He generally got

the selection ahead of two other contenders at that time, Mick Cowan and Bob Platt. Mel, from Huddersfield, was well over six feet, strong as an ox (in fact he was known as Bull) and took a fierce pride in playing for Yorkshire. He was, perhaps, underestimated by many of his contemporaries. Certainly his height and strength enabled him usually to get bounce and he could move it a bit, too. Perhaps what he lacked was a bit more of the killer instinct because as a cricketer he was a mild-mannered, almost gentle giant. Put him on a golf course and he became a different personality altogether. He would fight and argue over a game for half-a-crown with as much ferocity as any Ryder Cup man. Anyway, he fizzed out Frankie Worrell and Joey Carew with only 20 runs on the board which turned me loose on Kanhai and Nurse. In each innings I bowled Rohan with deliveries which I must have saved up for him for a long time.

Each one started off around the line of middle, or middle-and-leg, and each just clipped the top of the off stump. I was proud of both of them. Ken Taylor nipped in with three wickets from his little seamers and I had final figures of 5 for 37 in the West Indies total of 109. We declared our second innings at 145 for 6, setting the Windies 263 to win. Twelve minutes before lunch on the third day they were all out 151 and we had beaten the tourists by 111 runs. Five for 43 gave me match figures of 10 for 81 plus 75 runs for once out. The date was 17 May 1963: a day I remember with pride and a day I hope Yorkshire members will remember, too, when they next hear the horrifying suggestion which was going the rounds – that it's time Yorkshire joined the other sixteen first-class counties in signing an overseas professional. Never.

It's less than twenty years since we beat the West Indies, less than fifteen since we beat the Australians . . . full touring sides of experienced Test players. Why, then, should we bleat about other county sides with *two* overseas Test players having an unfair advantage over our homegrown lads? It's a shameful cry. If we cannot get together, from all the thousands of natural cricketers born in Yorkshire, a team to beat the other counties, then it's time to pack up. We have done it for nearly 120 years while the other counties have recruited from everywhere under the sun; we can do it again. It is not individual ability which has been missing in recent years so much as leadership on the one hand and a willingness to follow on the other. The first lesson a Yorkshire cricketer learned in my day was humility: a sense of belonging to something which had years of wonderful tradition behind it, something which was bigger than any individual player. We had our own personalities, it's true, and we expressed ourselves, projected those personalities, in different ways. But the common factor – that we would have given our lives for the side, and for each other in the cause of winning with that side – was the most important one of all. That common bond is, sadly, what has been missing from Yorkshire sides of the past decade. Instead, we have had a loose collection of individuals, some stars, some who have shone less brightly, but with single aims and ambitions, not a collective one. I make this point more than once in this book. It is not coincidence; it is not unconscious repetition.

17 The Greatest Ball

England v West Indies – Edgbaston, 1963

Of *Wisden*'s Five Cricketers of the Year 1963 no fewer than four were West Indian tourists – Charlie Griffith, Conrad Hunte, Rohan Kanhai and Gary Sobers. The fifth was my county captain, Brian Close, who had been battered black and blue in the second Test at Lord's after we had been given a fearful hammering by the Windies in the first at Old Trafford. Then came the drama of Lord's where the Test was finally drawn and where either side might have won in a marvellous finish. For the third, Philip Sharpe, another of my county colleagues and later a fellow member of the Yorkshire committee, was called up to a barrage of snide suggestions from the press that he must be the first man to get a Test place purely on fielding ability. If they had had a word with me I might have been able to suggest to them a list of names of players who went on MCC tours abroad who could neither bat, bowl, nor field! It's sufficient to answer such criticism by pointing out that quite apart from being the most outstanding slip-catcher in the country (and one of the best of all time), P. J. Sharpe averaged 46.23 in his twelve Tests. We can regard his seventeen catches as something of a bonus.

There had been a lot of rain before the match and Sobers provided more problems for our batsmen than Hall and Griffith. Nevertheless, 216 was a disappointing total and there was a lot of hard work ahead. We used only four bowlers and of those Tony Lock had just two overs of spin. The others were bowled by my opening partner Derek Shackleton, who was then thirty-eight years old, and Ted Dexter, who took 4 for 38 in

20 overs while I had 5 for 75 in 26 overs. In our second innings Sharpe hit 85 not out to indicate to those who didn't already know that he was not just a pretty catcher of the ball. On the last morning, Tony Lock had a merry thrash for 56 and Dexter set the West Indies to score 309 to win (or, more to the point, gave us four hours forty minutes to bowl them out, as far as I was concerned).

We started off well enough, removing both openers cheaply but then Kanhai, who had such a marvellous 1963 season, took root and got a lot of help from, first, Basil Butcher and then Joe Solomon.

Bearing in mind that Sobers was still to come, followed by the West Indies captain, Frankie Worrell, one or two anxious glances began to be cast towards the clock. It was then that I noticed that 'Shack', who was for so many years a master of swing and seam at a gentle medium pace, seemed to be coming off the pitch faster than I was and I began to cast around in the old memory bank. A game at Lord's, I remembered, had seen 'Typhoon' Tyson bowling in harness with David Smith, of Gloucestershire, a man of very much more friendly pace but a man who could move it around. And Smith had been faster off the pitch than Tyson. It seemed like an illusion at the time but I had seen it more than once on certain pitches and this looked like one of them.

I went on to the shorter run, which I was beginning to use quite a lot from time to time, used the seam, and suddenly the West Indies went to pieces. In four overs I took the last six wickets for four runs and those four came from Lance Gibbs' edged stroke between second and third slips when he came in at number eleven. Fifty-five minutes after lunch we had won by 217 runs and I now had another best-in-Tests analysis of 12 for 119. Now the record books show that I delivered 15,178 balls in my Test career and undoubtedly the best of them came in the first innings of this Edgbaston Test of 1963.

Garfield Sobers, like many other fine left-hand batsmen, was not always sure of the exact location of his off stump when a right-arm bowler was operating over the wicket and going wide of the crease. This was a ploy I often used because apart from everything else it gave you an extra fielder. With the ball coming across at a wide angle the wicketkeeper took the place usually occupied by first slip and it was possible to employ an extra gulley – an invaluable ally when the left-hand batsman drove at a ball which seemed to him to be well wide of the off stump. The slightest misjudgement, or a touch of movement, could so easily result in a thick outside edge to that finer gulley position. And this is what I was working on. Gary knew it and I knew that he knew it. So it became a battle of wits. I reasoned that as I set the field he would realize what was 'on' and, great player that he was, he would have to take some positive action to prove he was the master. Well, he didn't try it straight away . . .

I directed the ball right across him from wide of my crease and Gary decided, for the moment, to apply discretion. He shouldered arms to let the ball go through. And it bowled him.

Now if that ball had carried on along its normal line it would probably have passed nine inches wide of the off stump as Sobers quite rightly expected. But it didn't. It broke back and hit off and middle. I can see Sobers now, looking at the heavens with his lips pursed, asking himself what had happened. At the non-striker's end Frank Worrell gasped, 'I don't believe it.'

And the umpire hissing through his teeth, 'What a ball!'

Afterwards, Gary and Frankie got hold of me and demanded, 'F.S., how do you bowl that ball?'

I looked steadily at them, drew on my pipe and replied with what I hope was a suitably inscrutable expression, 'If I tell you that, you'll be looking for it next time. Sorry, fellers . . .'

Now I'll tell them, though. Or at least I'll reveal it to G. St Aubyn Sobers – Frankie, sadly, being no longer with us: I haven't the faintest idea. Did it hit a pebble, a tuft of loose earth? Had a bit of the seam become detached? Was it simply an act of God? I'll never know until I go to heaven. Or, if I go to the other place, I'll never know at all. But I remembered something Maurice Leyland once told me when I had bowled one in the nets which had come back from leg to off. I looked a bit puzzled and confessed that I didn't know how I'd done it. Maurice patted me on the shoulder and advised, 'Never try to find out, because if *you* don't know the batsman has no chance of knowing.'

I hope Richard Hutton reads this. I had a great affection for young Dick, who was a fine cricketer, and in his early days with Yorkshire he used to listen to people talking for a long time and then slip in a remark which was designed to be devastating – a real conversation stopper. He was listening to me talking about a bowling spell of which I was rather proud and I was giving it the full treatment, untainted by any false modesty. Richard waited his moment, then, as I paused for breath, he slipped in, 'Tell me, Fred – did you ever bowl a ball that merely went straight?'

The gallery waited. Surely, here was F.S. shot down at last. I was almost sorry to disappoint them. Calmly I turned to young Hutton and replied, 'Aye, lad. Three year ago. It were a long half-volley to Peter Marner and knocked the lot down.' So, Dick lad, if you ever hear me describing the greatest Test delivery I ever sent down, now you *can* have the last word.

18 The Hat Trick

Nottinghamshire v Yorkshire – Park Avenue, 1963

A hat trick is a nice achievement to have under the belt at any level of cricket. I can think of many fine bowlers, in first-class cricket and in other spheres, whose careers span twenty years without including a three-in-three. Let's face it – it takes some doing and you have either got to be very lucky or very good. It helps if you are both!

Every bowler has a favourite opposition, just as every batsman has. It usually starts with a good performance for no reason that you can quite put your finger on, then the memory of that performance helps a bit in your next encounter with the same side and before you know it you are looking forward to meeting them again. You can't wait to get at them. You *know* you are going to do well. You don't know *why* this is so; it just is. My favourite teams were Kent, Essex and Nottinghamshire.

The greatest favourite of these was Nottinghamshire and my special memory is not of one game against them but a composite of perhaps half a dozen matches. I honestly can't single one out because I had three hat tricks against Nottinghamshire, I took eight of their wickets on at least three occasions, and I got within a whisker of a totally unique record against them, too – which I'll come to in due course. In the meantime, let me say it was not a matter of a favourite ground because I enjoyed myself against them in places as far apart as Sheffield, Trent Bridge, Scarborough and Worksop.

The story of my love affair with Nottinghamshire starts at Trent Bridge on 21 July 1951 – the Benefit of Arthur Jepson, who was such a good trouper for Nottinghamshire in the post-war years and later went onto the first-class umpires' list. I was still pretty raw, midway through my second real season in the game, and if anyone had told me that Trent Bridge in the early fifties was a fast bowler's graveyard I don't suppose for one minute I would have taken a bit of notice. On the contrary, I might have said, 'Not for *this* fast bowler,' or something of the sort. I believed in myself; I believed I could bowl fast on any pitch; I had not yet learned to think my way through a game. Maybe that's why I seem to remember that the ball moved around a lot that day even though people who knew Trent Bridge extremely well in those days assure me that it is unlikely. The reputation of that pitch with bowlers of all kinds simply stank. They loathed it.

Even Harold Butler and Arthur Jepson used to groan at the mere thought of having to go out and bowl on it and Peter Harvey, the leg spinner, could usually bank on a raw spinning finger at the end of a day's bowling to a long line of defensive fieldsmen placed along the edge of the square. Faced with such fields, visiting batsmen no less than their bowlers grew to hate Trent Bridge and there was quite a shemozzle one Saturday afternoon in the early fifties when Wilf Wooller, one of the game's great characters, leading Glamorgan against Nottinghamshire, found himself completely immobilized. He didn't like it one little bit and Reg Simpson, who had *set* the defensive field, rubbed salt in the wound by bowling *underarm* to his rival skipper. Wooller, never slow to rise to a jibe of any kind, took an extremely poor view of the whole proceedings and the upshot of it all was a fine story for the Sunday papers.

That incident, of course, was still in the future when I opened the bowling on 21 July 1951, and the thought of a featherbed wicket never entered my mind. In fact, to this day I am completely certain the ball moved about so maybe we had different conditions that day, or perhaps the groundsman had left on some grass. Whatever the reason, Nottinghamshire, in Arthur Jepson's Benefit match, were 18 for 6 in no time at all. Bob Appleyard took the first wicket, I got the second and third, Norman Yardley the fourth and then came the first hat trick of my career: Reg Simpson and an amateur, A. K. Armitage (I've never been able to find any further mention of him in the reference books) were bowled and Peter Harvey caught behind. I ended with 8 for 53 and but for inexperience it would have been a better analysis than that – fewer runs conceded – but at least it was my career best up to that point. It overtook a return of 8 for 68 in a game against Nottinghamshire just a month earlier and after that game I was dropped! The competition for places was certainly tough in the early fifties. Bob Appleyard, for instance, was having his first full season in first-class cricket and he ended with exactly 200 wickets. Johnny Wardle had 122, I had 90 and Eddie Leadbeater (that rare Yorkshire animal, a leg spinner) had 81.

From a committee point of view, Bob Appleyard's success was a great thing because he was two bowlers in one. He could swing the new ball well and he could bowl cutters and genuine off spinners as well. So his success was not appreciated in quite the same way by the other bowlers fighting for places. (This was the side that never really achieved any team spirit for another seven or eight years and at the beginning of the decade there was fierce competition for places.)

In June 1951, at Bramall Lane, Sheffield, I didn't even get on first or second. The new ball was taken by Appleyard and shared by Johnny Whitehead who was genuinely quick. My 11 for 91 return in the match saw me dropped for the next match and from then until the end of August it was Cox and Box with Johnny and myself until, on 13 August, in the middle of a game in which I played a completely undistinguished role, I was awarded my cap.

Johnny Whitehead left the county at the end of the season. A fine fast bowler . . . and there just wasn't room for him. I had to wait four years for my next hat trick and to my delight it came on one of my favourite grounds – Scarborough – and this was the game which could have given me a unique record. In fact Norman Yardley, who was fielding close to the wicket at the time, does not understand why I don't have that record. In the first innings I had dismissed Ron Giles, Freddie Stocks and

Cyril Poole in consecutive deliveries. Hat trick number two. In the second innings I had Giles and Stocks in two balls (and that was a king pair for Freddie). But what must have been the thoughts going through Cyril Poole's mind as he came in to face a hat trick ball for the second time in the same game? It nipped back, hit him under the knee of the pad and we all went up. Not out, said the umpire, and Norman Yardley to this day does not know how the decision was reached. Now what a record that would have been! What a quiz question! And what a memory for Messrs Giles, Stocks and Poole to take round with them. Thirteen years later Neil Hawke was to reflect that as F. S. Trueman's 300th Test wicket, his name would be forever enshrined in the record books. Those three Nottinghamshire batsmen might well have been there as well.

Hat trick number three was by way of celebrating Ronnie Burnet's appointment as captain of Yorkshire. He led us for the first time in the traditional match against MCC at Lord's and my third hat trick came in that game. Number four might well have come in London, too, but at the Oval. An age-old tradition prevented it.

It was Alec Bedser's Benefit and somewhat to my surprise he was batting at number eleven. This made things a trifle tricky when he came out to bat – on a hat trick. I pondered the situation and as Alec arrived at the wicket I said to him, half-inquiringly (I was wishing someone would *tell* me what to do in the circumstances), 'One off the mark?'

Big Al replied, 'No, you go for your hat trick.' Well, if anything made up my mind it was that. If Alec could be big enough to forget about the tradition of giving a beneficiary one off the mark, I could certainly be big enough to insist on the ancient rite being observed.

I told him, 'No, Alec. A tradition's a tradition. You *get* one off the mark.' The field went back, I bowled a long half volley at medium pace, and Alec pushed it for a single. Honour was done. The trouble was he and Jim Laker (the last pair) went on to get about 50 apiece.

It doesn't always work out as felicitously. Philip Sharpe, in *his* Benefit match, was out for 0. There aren't many recorded cases of that. But he chose the Roses game and in the heat of battle Peter Lever forgot all about the occasion, bowled Sharpie a nasty lifter and he was caught out before scoring. How unlucky can you get? But by and large the traditions are always observed and I think it's right that they should be. It always seems to me that the crowd enjoy them and certainly they joined in with a sense of pleasure which seemed to engulf everyone, players and spectators alike, in the Bedser Benefit.

Getting back to Nottinghamshire, there was one more eight-wicket performance to come, and one more hat trick. The eight wickets came at Worksop on 12 July 1962, and the analysis (8 for 84) is a bit unusual in that after Yorkshire had batted for most of the first day. Nottinghamshire lost one of their openers to Tony Nicholson very cheaply and then that great character Norman Hill together with Mervyn Winfield stayed until the close. I had no wicket for 49 and I wasn't very pleased with life.

I went out with a mate that evening, called to see some of my old friends just over the border in South Yorkshire and got to bed in the early hours. Next day I was a different bowler – eight for 35 and six of those came off one of Bomber Wells' 'special' strokes. Bomber must have been the finest number eleven who ever lived. His batting technique to anything above medium pace was admirably simple. He took one step back, in the direction of the square-leg umpire and waved the bat in a scything motion. He added a new dimension to the tradition of hitting 'on the up', and he caught one of mine on this occasion. It sailed backward of point, cleared the privet hedge and landed on the bowling green – six runs.

Looking back on that brief but spectacular innings of the Bomber, his 11 runs must have run pretty close to being his career best; certainly double figures were rare for him. But again, he was one of the great characters of the game and cricket's legend and folklore would be the poorer if B. D. Wells had never stepped upon the stage.

That leaves us with the hat trick of 1963. Geoff Millman was the first victim off the last ball of my fifteenth over at Park Avenue on 14 August 1963; Ian Davison was caught off the first ball of the next and then came the moment of sweet revenge for the previous season's indignities at Worksop – B. D. Wells, b Trueman, 0. You can't hit straight yorkers over backward point!

Oh Mr Trueman. There's a gentleman from the Press wearing an asbestos suit who'd like your views on Keith Miller's assertion that you're BURNED OUT.
VISITORS DRESSING ROOM
MULLYETT.

19 The 300th Wicket

England v Australia – The Oval, 1964

My friendship with Neil Hawke started on England's 1962–3 tour to Australia. Hawkie and I simply seemed to 'get on' together. We enjoyed a few drinks and did a lot of chatting and one evening I rang him at the Australians' hotel and said, 'I've been lucky enough to get four tickets for a concert by Nat 'King' Cole. Brian Statham, Noddy Pullar and myself are going. Would you like the other ticket?'

Neil replied, 'The taxi's leaving now, mate.' So the four of us enjoyed that lovely smooth, silky voice.

Years later Hawkie said to me, 'D'you know – when the news came of Nat's death I sat down and thought about that night the four of us went to hear him together.'

My reply was immediate. 'That's just what I did, too.'

So the Hawk and I were really pretty good mates when he toured England with Bobby Simpson's 1964 Australians. Later we became even greater friends when he settled for several years in the North of England, became a successful businessman, got his golf handicap down to one, gave a great deal of help to a talented young amateur, Hogan Stott, and put Nelson Golf Club on the map during his spell as captain of that Lancashire club.

Round about the same time, Peter Parfitt had retired from the captaincy of Middlesex and was developing a tiny country pub (near my home in the Yorkshire Dales) into a beautifully appointed restaurant. And as my friend and Test Match Special commentary colleague Don Mosey comes from that area and still has his roots there, the four of us developed a strong quadrilateral association. But at the end of the 1970s Neil underwent so much major surgery that, by now back home in his native South Australia, he became a clinical miracle. He was literally carved to pieces in an Adelaide hospital, was written off for dead half a dozen times, but with the help of the lady he subsequently married, Beverley, he retained the will to live and somehow survived it all. Soon the letters, witty and ever-humorous, were flying across the world to the other three of us. A truly remarkable man, N. J. N. Hawke.

Let's slip back now to the Kennington Oval on Saturday, 15 August 1964.

After the third Test, at Headingley, I needed three wickets to complete 300 Test victims. For years people had said it couldn't be done because far fewer Tests were played then than today when on every day of the year one or more seems to be going on somewhere in the world. Up to that point, I had played in sixty-four Tests and I hope I may be forgiven for reflecting a little gloomily on what might have been if I hadn't missed out on tours to Australia and South Africa, and thinking about the times I had been dropped in England after performances which in the 1980s would apparently merit automatic selection for a whole series. Just three wickets needed and I was dropped for Old Trafford!

Perhaps it wasn't such a bad thing after all because Fred Rumsey came in to learn about Test wickets the hard way; he and John Price toiled away on an absolute beauty at Old Trafford where Bobby Simpson got a treble hundred. So I was back for the final Test at the Oval and the newspapers made sure that no one in the whole country was unaware of what was required to put me very firmly in the record books.

We won the toss, batted and made only 182 as Hawkie took 6 for 47 and the Aussies then set out on the slow grind to put themselves in an unassailable position. We had reached late morning on the third day and I think Ted Dexter was getting pretty desperate as he cast about for an idea of what to do next. His eye fell on Peter Parfitt and I could see that his idea was to try a bit of what Parf has always been pleased to call off spin.

Now it was Richard Hutton, of the laconic but pointed wit, who once summed up Peter's bowling. Parf had recently been appointed to the Lord's 'chucking' committee which investigated and ruled upon suspect bowling actions. Richard looked at him with lofty and incredulous disdain. 'Parf,' he said, 'for you to sit on that committee is the equivalent of Adolf Hitler presiding at the Nuremberg Trials.' It's an epigram which Parf himself loves to recall, accompanied by the best-known chuckle in world cricket.

So as the skipper turned the idea over in his mind I made up mine. 'Give me that bloody ball,' I snarled, just about snatching it from Ted's grasp. And I put myself on to bowl off the short run, cutting the ball rather than swinging it, at something a bit above medium pace. I got one to nip back and it bowled Ian Redpath. In came 'Garth' McKenzie and Colin Cowdrey caught him first ball.

High up in the top regions of the Oval pavilion there was a sudden scramble in the Aussie dressing room. As Redpath and Tom Veivers had ground inexorably on through the morning there had been the usual complement of 'kippers', a card school, the punters going through the *Sporting Life* for the most likely means of improving finances during the afternoon. There was no urgency. The Poms were being sorted out and a lead of 200 plus was in prospect. Suddenly F.S. was in sight of his 300th Test wicket and who had to go to the middle on a hat trick? N. J. N. Hawke. He threw on his pads, didn't even glance at the clock and was hobbling down the stairs (a lot of them at the Oval) still fumbling with his straps when he met the England side coming in . . . for lunch.

So I had to sit through forty minutes with a cup of tea thinking about 300 Test wickets and possibly the fifth hat trick of my career. One floor above, Hawkie's thoughts went like this, 'Well, I suppose this is my best chance to get into the record book. No one's ever going to remember me for what I have done in Test cricket but the man who becomes Fred's 300th Test victim will be remembered for all time.' (That, incidentally, is a typical Hawke thought. He was a genuinely modest player in his own mind but he was a damn good one for all that.)

The interval passed very slowly but at last it was ten past two and we were all out in the middle again. The 'hat trick' ball went harmlessly past the off stump and Hawkie barely gave it a glance. He settled and batted on while 16 runs were added (getting 14 of them himself) before I got one to move away and it was Hawke, c Cowdrey (first slip) b Trueman – my 300th Test victim. Neil was the first to congratulate me. He walked down the pitch, grinned at me and said, 'Well done, mate. I should be all right for the champagne now, eh?'

'Too right you are,' I replied as the England players added their congratulations. It was a great moment, one that will remain in my memory as long as I live. Lance Gibbs was to pass my final figure of 307 Tests wickets and good luck to him, but no one can ever take from me the knowledge that I was the first to reach 300. They said it couldn't be done and that streak of cussedness which is so much a part of me was determined that it could. A lot of toil and sweat had gone into achieving it. If there were blood and tears, too, they were not mine. When my final total was ultimately beaten it was by a *slow* bowler and in twelve Tests more.

Lance took two more wickets than I did and they cost him on an average 7½ runs more than mine. His striking rate was around one every 90 balls; mine nearer one every 50. If it is immodest for me to voice such matters then I'll plead guilty to that because I am proud of that record, *bloody* proud.

Just as in 1953 success at the Oval had been tinged with the sadness of my grandmother's death, now on the same ground came a blow of a different kind. I now learned that I had been left out of the side to tour South Africa. I missed eleven Tests under Len Hutton's captaincy after our return from the West Indies tour of 1953–4 and played in only three of the next fifteen after Peter May became skipper. I had been dropped – to me somewhat inexplicably – in the series at home and here were another five Tests in which I might have played as well as visiting a country I badly wanted to see.

Instead, I went to the West Indies with the Rothman Cavaliers and though that was a happy tour I could not resist searching around for whatever news I could find from South Africa. When I saw the details of the fifth Test in Port Elizabeth I nearly choked. John Price had broken down and Somerset's Kenny Palmer (who was coaching out there) had been called up to open the bowling with Ian Thomson of Sussex. Ian Thomson and Kenny Palmer opening England's attack in a Test, I couldn't believe my eyes; good lads both, good honest county bowlers. But Test players? Never in a million years.

So in middle age I occasionally brood upon what might have been. In twenty more Tests, which I might very conceivably have played, it is not impossible that my Test victims might have got near to the 400 mark. It would have needed not many more than two wickets an innings, and I can't help remembering that most of the Tests I missed were when I was in my early and middle twenties. Do I blame myself? Let's put it this way: if I had known then what I know now about keeping my nose clean I might to some extent have been a different sort of chap. If I had thought, 'Watch it. Someone's storing up a bit of hate for you. You are going to miss Tests, and all that they involve,' then I might have followed a bit more closely what was then defined as the straight and narrow path of international cricket righteousness.

And then I ask myself, 'But would I have been the same bowler if Fiery Fred had been rather more Friendly Fred?' My bowling was made up of more than an action which kept me bowling fast for twenty seasons, more than the time and study I gave to all great bowlers of my day and the days before me, more than snorting, fuming hostility towards batsmen. It was a combination of all these ingredients and perhaps I might have been a lesser bowler without any one of them or with a less generous measure of all of them. Perhaps I needed a father figure, as Mike Brearley suggested of Ian Botham in the summer of 1981. I don't know. I *do* know that I would desperately have liked to play in those twenty or more Tests I missed.

The Aussies open their tour at Worcester

20 The Ultimate Pleasure

Yorkshire v The Australians – Sheffield, 1968

Of all the matches in which I captained Yorkshire none gave me anything approaching the pleasure of that victory over the touring Australians at Bramall Lane, Sheffield, on 2 July 1968. I had been skipper when Yorkshire beat the Indians and when we had given the Pakistanis the fright of their lives, I had been in the side which beat the West Indian tourists of 1963 . . . we very nearly had a nap hand. But no Yorkshire side had beaten the Australians since 1902 and as I was captain in the absence of Brian Close I wanted a win very badly indeed. Closey hadn't done it, Norman Yardley hadn't done it, Brian Sellers hadn't – no one had for sixty-six years. But Yorkshire was a powerful side in 1968 and the Aussies paid us the compliment of turning out a very strong side indeed – Lawry, Redpath, Walters, Sheahan, Ian Chappell (on his first tour), Inverarity, Taber, McKenzie, Gleeson, Connolly and Renneberg. But we reckoned in those days that a Yorkshire side was a match for any touring team and I was aiming at nothing short of an outright win.

I won the toss and we batted. The match was played in warm, at times muggy, weather and the bowlers always had some help, but we batted very solidly indeed. The lowest score amongst the first five was 33 and when Australia took the second new ball about an hour before close of play I was a bit surprised and disappointed that Lawry placed a third man and a deep fine leg. Bill was always a dour and defensive-minded cricketer but I felt at this stage that if he attacked he had a reasonable chance of getting us out before the close.

Alternatively, with attacking fields we had a chance of knocking a few quick runs and I could think about a declaration. So we batted through to the close and on the second morning I passed the Aussies at the nets and Lawry, with his pads on, inquired, 'I presume you've declared?'

'No,' I replied. 'Why should I? We're batting on.'

There was a committee meeting that morning and as I went in, Brian Sellers, the chairman, asked, 'What are you going to do?'

'We're carrying on,' I answered. 'I want to get 350 or 360 and try to bowl them out twice. That wicket will turn later on.'

'Fair enough,' said the chairman. We completed the meeting and I put on my pads and went out with Ray Illingworth who had battled it out overnight. We got to 355 for nine when I declared, giving us half an hour's bowling before lunch so the shine was still going to be there after the break. We would get two bites at the cherry.

Things started to go our way and the lads fielded magnificently. There has never been anything, in my experience, like the Yorkshire side during those days in the field when we were trying to force a win. Their cricket was tigerish. With the help of some magnificent catching we got the tourists out for 148 in spite of Lawry's splendid innings of 58. He really did bat extremely well but I knew that if we got him out in the second innings we could win.

At the end of the Aussie innings the groundsman asked me which roller I wanted and I suggested he should address his question to the Australian captain. Then, to make sure there was no misunderstanding, I went into the Australian dressing room to say, 'Will you bat again, Bill, please?' Now this was prompted, and I still have to laugh at the memory of it, by a gigantic cock-up which had occurred two years earlier, in Yorkshire's match against the Indians, again at Bramall Lane. I was enforcing the follow-on on that occasion and I thought a signal to their captain, the Nawab of Pataudi, was sufficient indication of my intention. The Noob misunderstood the signal, thought I wanted him to take the field, so after an interval of ten minutes (during which no roller at all was applied) both teams found themselves coming down the steps and out onto the ground . . . side by side! It was a *right* cock-up, and everyone had to go back, laughing like hell, while the pitch was rolled for the Indians. So I made sure *that* didn't happen again.

At least it gave us another ten minutes in which to prime ourselves. I told the lads simply, 'We can win this. Just let's get stuck into them. Play like you did in the first innings and we'll do it.' As I have said, it was a good Aussie side but one or two of the players like Paul Sheahan and Ian Chappell were unused to English conditions. Now Bill Lawry was a very fine player with a quite magnificent defence. He always seemed as though he could bat right through a match unless something very unusual happened and while I knew we could keep winkling them out at the other end, Lawry was the man who could hold us up.

I was determined that no one, and nothing, was going to prevent a Yorkshire win over the Australians. It was Dick Hutton who started us on the road to it by producing a magnificent delivery to Lawry. It started on or just outside the off stump and looked like being a long half-volley. It turned out to be a yorker which swung late and hit the bottom of the leg stump; Lawry b Hutton, 0. We were on our way and the crowd, almost to a man, jumped in the air. Hutton had, in effect, opened up *both* ends.

The third morning was dark and threatening and there was rain about. I thought, 'Oh no, not that.' As the light deteriorated I brought Ray Illingworth on and I bowled Geoff Boycott a bit at the other end to forestall any appeals against the light with the faster bowlers in action. The light improved, Hutton and I got rid of the first four batsmen and Raymond polished off the rest. Australia all out 138; we had won by an innings and 69 runs – Yorkshire's first victory over an Aussie touring side since 1902. The crowds poured in that morning as they have rarely done for the third day of a first-class match. One man I know couldn't stand it in his office in Manchester so he jumped into his car, drove over the Pennines and arrived to see us leaving the field. He did get a celebration drink, though. I went into the dressing room and said, 'Right lads, order whatever you want.'

The champagne flowed and we knew that the whole of Yorkshire rejoiced with us and for us because Yorkshire cricket is a very personal thing to everyone born within the broad acres. We were conscious of this; it is something every Yorkshire player used to know and to understand. We were heirs to a tremendous legacy and we accepted that with pride as well as gratitude. But best of all was the feeling of utter satisfaction within the dressing room which only truly comes from a whole-hearted team effort. We knew we had done it as a team in the best sense of the word, and if I allowed myself to bask a little in reflected glory it was glory which reflected from a team – my team.

I emphasize all this because I firmly believe that it was that team effort, that team spirit, which won the match. It's a bit of a cliché, I know, but no less of a fact for that.

Team spirit is something which is perhaps better defined when it is absent as it seems to have been sadly absent from Yorkshire's dressing room for more than a decade. In the team of the sixties it might be reasonably said that there were considerably more top names than there have been since but we did not look at it that way. There were no stars as far as we were concerned. In Dumas' words, it was one for all and all for one and that was literally true. Peter Stringer, a second-teamer who took part in that win over the Australians, got the same match money as I did – his captain and a man who had played in sixty-seven Tests – and that was right. Differentials which have crept in have not helped team spirit and it can be cogently argued that they have been a major factor in destroying it.

If anyone – *anyone* – in a side of those days had shown the slightest sign of developing a prima donna complex either Closey, Illy, Jimmy Binks or myself would have sorted it out at once because no one was bigger than the team. Closey missed that game in a season when he had a lot of injury and illness problems but he was as delighted as anyone who had taken part. He wasn't jealous because he had not led the side; he was absolutely delighted. Brian has talked a lot of rubbish and a lot of wisdom in his time and one of the wisest remarks he ever made was this: captaincy is about *giving*. You have to give something of yourself not just to the team as a unit but to every individual member who might need help, or advice or encouragement. Any captain who thinks about taking even the least particle of credit from what his side has achieved is not a captain.

These are my thoughts as I look backwards from retirement. They are prompted by some of the sad events which have overtaken Yorkshire cricket since those heady days of the sixties. But of that day at Bramall Lane, Sheffield, in 1968, I can only reflect that in a long career, full of wonderful moments, it represented the ultimate pleasure.

SUNDAY CRICKET AT LORD'S.
For what I am about to receive give me middle and leg
ROY ULLYETT

21 The Farmers' Boys

Cracoe v Linton – Cracoe, Yorkshire Dales, 1979

I have often thought it a pity that no one has ever done for village cricket in the North of England what A. G. McDonnell did for it in the South. We have our blacksmiths and our vicars, our retired military gentlemen and our lords of the manor, all of whom make a contribution to the gentle eccentricity of a game which yields nothing to the Test arena in the passion with which it is played.

'England, *my* England,' began amongst the mine-workings of South Yorkshire; little did I think it would in due course move to the glorious countryside of the West Riding Dales where the legends may vary in their idiom but are no less hallowed for that. No coloured caps and cucumber sandwiches here. Rollers, heavy or otherwise, are a refinement unknown to most clubs of the Dales Evening League. Evening cricket is a necessity in such parts because most teams consist, in the main, of lads from the farms of beautiful Wharfedale, and to a farmer there is no Saturday or Sunday – just another day when the milking and the mucking out has to be done as it has on the other five. Occasionally, afternoon friendlies have been essayed but invariably a crisis arises in the ranks as milking-time comes round and one or more of the participants realizes that there is no stand-in back at the farm. The story goes around Grassington way that, as a second innings ground rather slowly along its course, one of the fielding side (after a series of anxious inquiries about the time from spectators), grabbed the ball himself and rolled over the opposition with slow left-arm deliveries which his team-mates had never seen before so that he could get back to his lowing herd by six o'clock. Necessity is indeed the mother of invention in rural cricket.

Preparation of pitches is a matter of superb improvisation, as the BBC's Northern Symphony Orchestra cricket team found on arrival at the village of Cracoe. Four men, shoulder to shoulder, were slowly and solemnly walking to and fro across twenty-two yards of a hillside, treading down the grass of the meadow to form the pitch. I was not aware of this piece of local history when I was invited to play for the Cracoe village side . . .

As I mention elsewhere, I have always had a deep affection for the countryside, and after my retirement from the first-class game I made my home in an idyllic spot in a tiny hamlet between the valleys of the Aire and the Wharfe. In my walled garden I get enormous pleasure from watching the variety of the birdlife and I know that a long cavalcade of guests have shared my pleasure in a post-breakfast cup of tea on the lawn, watching the tits and the finches, the robins, a family of goldcrests, even a tree creeper. Beyond the bottom of the garden is a stream bordered by birch, ash, elm and alder – home to a dozen other species as the waterside is to the kingfisher. And rising above the trees, the bracken-clad slopes of Sharphaw hill where the young grouse camouflage themselves from an army of natural foes before facing the guns of the August marksmen. It's my own little bit of heaven.

A mile or two up the road is my local, the Angel, and just beyond that the more recent home of Cracoe Cricket Club since their move from the field beyond the Devonshire Arms where the light of battle once glinted in the eyes of the BBC Northern Symphony Orchestra's fast bowler. I moved to that particular blessed plot in the belief that my cricket would henceforward be confined to benefit matches, charity games and the odd appearance with MCC sides playing against public schools. There were invitations from League clubs to join them but my Saturdays were going to be spent watching sport for the *Sunday People* so League cricket was impracticable. No – my home was going to be the one place where I could relax totally. I had not heard of the Dales Evening League . . .

Scarcely had I downed my first drink in my new local than I was approached by the lads of the village with the news that, as I was now an ecclesiastical parishioner, I was qualified to play for their club. Foolishly, I told them, 'Right. Well, if I can help you out any time, just give me a shout.'

In two weeks the call came. The match was at Grassington, far bigger than Cracoe and in fact the 'capital' of Upper Wharfedale. We won. Now a Yorkshireman will go to greater lengths to indicate that he is unimpressed than any other bloke on earth. The vanquished 'Gerstoners' solemnly assured me that their star player was unavailable that evening, otherwise there would have been a different tale to tell. I rose to the bait as readily as I had gobbled it thirty years earlier when the Sheffield League visitors to Roche Abbey had looked merely to their opening pair to knock off 43 runs for victory. 'Oh aye,' I responded. 'We'll see about that.' And I asked our skipper when the next game was scheduled. It was a home match.

Our opponents were Linton, a beautiful little spot grouped around a village green just three miles from Cracoe. Our wicket is a far cry from the jute matting of Trinidad. One ball would shoot straight along the ground, the next leap over the heads of batsman and wicketkeeper after pitching on exactly the same spot. (I have heard wickets described as 'unpredictable' in the Test Match Special commentary box and permitted myself a quiet smile. My colleague who said that had no experience of the Dales Evening League.) One ball went through at a height somewhere between the two extremes – a six byes is not unknown in those parts – hit the wicketkeeper between the eyes and broke his spectacles. And the skipper, who was beginning to look a bit embarrassed, asked me sheepishly, 'Would you mind taking a rest? I know you've still two of your six overs to bowl but, er . . .'

'I understand,' I said. 'Certainly.' The scoreboard read: Linton – 9 for 7 wickets, and I had taken 5 for none. As I retired, a new batsman took the field and somewhat to my surprise he wore brown trousers and matching suede shoes. He laid about him mightily, was top scorer with 11, and we were left to make 23 to win which enabled us to patronize the bar of the local for an hour longer than was usually the case. Here I learned that the brown-trousered maestro was on a caravan holiday in the village. He had never played cricket in his life but he had heard of me, bless him, and had volunteered to make up the numbers, when Linton found themselves a man short, so he could play against F. S. Trueman.

It was a bit disappointing to find that the opposition, far from appreciating an extra hour's drinking time (and discreetly avoiding any reference to fielding an unregistered player who had made half their runs) took a decidedly poor view of my appearance in the Cracoe ranks. A deputation of three waited upon me in the bar and without any beating about the bush announced, 'You should not be allowed to play against us. You have played for Yorkshire and you have played Test cricket and it's not right for us to have to face you.'

Well, here was the other extreme from the unimpressionable lads of Dales cricket. Mildly, I pointed out, 'I'm forty-eight years old, you know, and I don't get all that much chance to practise.'

'Never mind that,' was the inflexible response. 'You shouldn't be allowed to play.' The matter was taken to the League, a meeting was held and it was decreed that I could not play again for Cracoe until I was fifty! That day has come and gone but I have not yet been invited to make my comeback in the Dales Evening League.

It was all a bit of fun, not least the solemnly reached judgement about my future eligibility, but I couldn't help pointing out to the deputation in the bar that evening that the best way of improving one's game is to play against better opposition. But let no one ever knock village cricket to me, despite the righteous anger of defeated Linton. If there were no village cricket there would be no feeder service to League cricket. If we didn't have good Leagues there would be no Minor Counties cricket, to the acute discomfort of the county game, and, in time, Test cricket. Every level has its part to play and every part makes up the whole. The whole is something which may be 'only a game'. But what a game.

22 The Last Drop

Courage Old England XI v England Ladies XI – Bath, 1981

The idea of getting together a team of former Test players to stage matches for charity had been in the back of my mind for several years. So many present-day cricket stars are overseas players and, without wanting in any way to get into one of those 'things ain't what they used to be' debates, I had felt for a long time that a turn out of some of the great players of the fifties and sixties might have a certain appeal to a generation of cricket lovers to whom these chaps were merely names or statistics; it would also give older followers of the game an opportunity for a bit of nostalgia.

I had thought about it a great deal but I hadn't done anything positive to get it off the ground until one day, cracking a bottle of champagne in El Vino's, in Fleet Street, with the veteran cricket writer Reg Hayter, I mentioned the idea. Reg said, 'Let me take a note of that. I might just have someone willing to back you.' Off he went, and in the autumn of 1980 I found myself attending a meeting with David Wynne-Morgan, a public relations expert, and the Courage Old England XI was born.

My contemporaries, and a few even more golden oldies, welcomed the idea enthusiastically and in no time at all I had a pool of thirty-four players to choose from. There was no shortage of applications for fixtures with us, either, and by arranging matches on a fairly widespread geographical basis we were able to make sure every volunteer got a game. We had all managed to keep ourselves reasonably fit in the fifteen or more years since we had finished playing; even so there were a few creaking fifty-year-old joints, and some aching sixty-year-old muscles from time to time, before the summer of 1981 was over. And as Courage paid a fee to each of its gladiators, two of our most venerable members actually surrendered their amateur status at the age of sixty-one; Mr R. T. Simpson (Nottinghamshire and England) and Mr D. V. Brennan (Yorkshire and England), both born in 1920, at last became simple mercenaries like the rest of us: Simpson, R. T. and Brennan, D. V.! As the captain of this illustrious band, I was never short of advice on the field either. Brian Close alone would have been quite enough when it came to telling me what to do but I had a few years of that during my playing days so now it was my turn!

At various times we found three or four different people setting the field in addition to the captain and the bowler, each of them burning with enthusiasm and absolutely confident in the knowledge that *he* knew precisely what was required. Sadly, forty years on, muscles and reflexes don't always work or respond in the same way and thus, in a game at Smethwick, with the opposition needing a couple of runs to win off the last ball, there was a conference about how that ball should be delivered – a conference which would have made a United Nations debate sound like meditation time in a Trappist monastery. Darkness had virtually fallen by the time the field had been set and I had sifted through all the advice which had been pressed upon me. *I* knew what was required; *I* had no doubts at all about what I was going to bowl.

In I ran and delivered . . . a full toss. It whistled back over my head for a straight six and we had lost. I grabbed my sweater, and as we trudged mournfully off the field with a chorus of, 'What the hell did you bowl that for?' ringing in my ears, I paused for a moment, like a stag at bay, and recognized the dreadful truth.

'Twenty years ago, my old flower,' I snarled at the nearest of my critics, 'that would have been a swinging yorker and it would have knocked his bloody hob down.' Alas, at fifty, the spirit may be willing but the flesh can be treacherously weak.

With such debates and such enthusiasms, we played through the summer of '81 with immeasurable delight, getting as much fun from our arguments as our cricket. A procession of great players crossed our stage . . . Compton, Graveney, Milburn, D'Oliveira, Lewis, Sharpe, Rhodes, Allen, Titmus, Evans and John Edrich. Individual performances might at times have smacked more of an ageing Donald Wolfit than a youthful Ivor Novello but there was no doubt at all about the overall appeal to the public. The crowds flocked in. So that when the request came to stage a match against the England Ladies XI to help them raise funds for their tour to New Zealand, middle-aged macho was suddenly allied to cricketing zeal. We none of us can ever quite accept that the sex appeal of our salad days has entirely forsaken us. D. C. S. Compton might not sell a million jars of Brylcreem today if he were to dig his RAF uniform out of mothballs and beam at us from the hoardings, but don't tell him that. We are all as we imagine ourselves to be.

And so the prospect of battle with a group of nubile maidens had the double appeal of helping a worthwile cause (and we nobly reflected that this, first and foremost, was our aim) and getting to grips in the nicest possible way with the flower of cricketing womanhood.

The game was played at the Lansdowne Club, in Bath. My old pal, Rachael Heyhoe-Flint, skippered the Ladies and by arrangement we batted first. John Jameson and Arthur Milton found the opening over, bowled by Sarah Potter, the twenty-year-old daughter of TV playwright Dennis ('Pennies from Heaven') Potter, rather interesting. Sarah, apart from being a bit of a beauty, bowls off a 24-yard run and after respectfully conceding a maiden over to her, Milt vouchsafed to his partner the information that 'they were swinging'. Rachael, whose salty humour has enlivened many an otherwise all-male cricket evening, overheard this and innocently inquired whether Arthur was referring to the bowling. (Rachael it was who described professional coaching as a man trying to get you to keep your legs close together when other men had spent a lifetime trying to get them wide apart.)

Miss Potter's new ball partner was Cathy Mowat, a

Are you sure this can prove if I bowl with a straight arm?
NZ WOMEN'S CRICKET TOUR
ROY ULLYETT.

tri-lingual secretary from London, who conceded eight in her first over but got revenge when John Jameson miscued a hook to mid-wicket and was caught by the Ladies' captain, resplendent in a two-tone blue head bandeau of the Dennis Lillee variety. Milton was caught in the gulley off Glynis Hullah, a medium-pace seamer, and the opening pair were back in the hutch for 38, which brought together two of the greatest heart-throbs ever to wear an England cap – Tony Lewis and Basil D'Oliveira. Clearly they enjoyed their company out in the middle to such an extent that restive mutterings began to be heard around the pavilion about 'those two hogging it, as usual'. At 99, Lewis went for a six hit and was magnificently caught after a dive as graceful as it was courageous by Jan Southgate.

Enter Compo . . . a great sentimental moment which brought tears to the eyes of many a grandmother in the 2500 crowd. Gallant to the end, he faced seven deliveries before bowing to the off-spinning expertise of Carole Hodges, a Midland Bank clerk from Poulton-le-Fylde. Dick Richardson hit a skier to such a height that when the fielders reached Sarah Potter to congratulate her on holding the catch she was still white with fear. Meanwhile, Dolly (whose caveman approach to womankind has always been in contrast to, say, the smoother charms of A. R. Lewis) was now dispatching the bowling to all parts.

It was the unkindest cut, drive and hook because women bowl with a five-ounce ball and Basil's hitting cost them £28 to replace two which he hit completely out of sight – not the kindliest of gestures to a crowd of girls trying to raise the cost of their fares to New Zealand. I joined Basil for a stand of 40 in thirteen minutes and then was ever so slightly staggered to see young Jan Southgate, the civil servant who *wasn't* on a go-slow, stretch to her left in the covers to hold a catch off one of the best-timed strokes I have ever played . . . a bit useful those England Ladies.

We totalled 209 for 7 and for the start of the Ladies' innings I'll let Tom Graveney take up the story. (The game was played on the Sunday of the Oval Test Match v Australia and Tom, who was out of action for us with a broken finger, switched from his TV Test commentary to the public address system at Lansdowne.)

'I have always regarded fast bowlers as thick. No disrespect to my captain, of course, but really new-ball bowlers have never impressed me as being amongst the brightest members of the human race. If I needed any evidence to support the view, it was provided by Dusty Rhodes on this occasion. Fred opened the bowling and Dusty took over at the other end. He only ambled in for two or three yards but then let it go like a thunderbolt. Stumps went flying in all directions and numbers two and three in the order were back in the pavilion before he had finished his first over. "Come off it, Dusty," was the cry from all sides, so he bowled a couple of gentle leg breaks to Rachael, the number four, and then let another one go. Again, the stumps scattered all over the place and the England Ladies were 5 for 3 with three leading batsmen bowled Rhodes for 0. He was promptly banished to the outfield, never to return, and quite right, too.'

Well, that's the Graveney view. I'm not going to agree with his opinion about fast bowlers in general, of course, but there are times when he may have a point. We all got along a lot better with Fred Titmus and David Allen bowling and there was a scramble for the short-leg fielding position. Men I have known to turn white during their playing careers at the thought of fielding closer to the bat than deep mid-off were suddenly shouldering each other out of the way to get a place in the off spinners' leg-traps! I suppose a well-rounded bottom, only partially concealed beneath a neat pleated skirt, does bring out certain primitive stirrings.

Somehow Fred Titmus got himself in there alongside Tony Lewis (naturally *he'd* be there) when D. A. Allen was bowling and he noticed the lady batsman's thigh pad emerging from beneath her skirt as she bent over her stance at the wicket. Now Fred is just a little bit deaf and what he imagines to be a whisper usually emerges as a bellow which would make a toastmaster or an RSM green with envy. He now 'whispered' to A. R. Lewis, not without a certain degree of natural excitement, 'Hey, her knickers are coming down.'

A scarlet-hued batsman straightened up as if he had actually pinched her bottom, one horrified hand stretching round to check her equipment. With a dignity which had no impact whatsoever on the two lecherous crouchers she informed them, 'They most certainly are not.'

Godfrey Evans, behind the timbers, found himself in a privileged position as well, and was clearly quite fascinated by the shapely charms of Jackie Court, a Sports Centre secretary from Ealing. He had plenty of time to indulge himself because Jackie hit 27, but the batting fireworks came from Glynis Hullah who scored 63 not out, including 26 off the last eight balls she received and two huge sixes off the final over bowled by David Allen. So the Ladies finished at 158 for 8, scored in 100 minutes (despite the now-disgraced Rhodes!) and modesty demands that I leave the final word to my rival captain:

'In all fairness it is very difficult for women to compete with men on equal terms as far as cricket is concerned. Praise be that Freddie Trueman played the game in the right spirit!'